THE BIG BOOK OF
SPY TRIVIA

SPY STORIES, SECRET AGENT FACTS, AND ESPIONAGE SKILLS FROM HISTORY'S GREATEST COVERT MISSIONS

BERNADETTE JOHNSON

ULYSSES PRESS

Published in the US by:
ULYSSES PRESS
PO Box 3440
Berkeley, CA 94703
www.ulyssespress.com

ISBN: 978-1-64604-130-5
Library of Congress Control Number: 2020946968

Printed in the United States by Kingery Printing Company
10 9 8 7 6 5 4 3 2 1

Acquisitions editor: Claire Sielaff
Managing editor: Claire Chun
Project editor: Bridget Thoreson
Editor: Renee Rutledge
Proofreader: Mark Rhynsburger
Front cover design: Rebecca Lown
Icons: © davooda/shutterstock.com

IMPORTANT NOTE TO READERS: Although the author and publisher have made every effort to ensure that the information in this book was correct at press time, the author and publisher do not assume and hereby disclaim any liability to any party for any loss, damage, or disruption caused by errors or omissions, whether such errors or omissions result from negligence, accident, or any other cause.

To Jeff and Molly for all the support and snuggles.

CONTENTS

INTRODUCTION

In many ways, the history of spying is the history of everything, so inextricable is espionage from the machinations of power that have shaped our world. But there is a great deal we don't know about this topic. The thing about espionage is—it's covert. Those in the trade aim to remain undiscovered. So there is no telling the number of operations (successful or otherwise) about which we'll never know the details.

Fortunately for us, there is no shortage of examples we do know about. And we learn more daily. We won't discover some spy stories until they are declassified decades later. Some will get leaked or broken by the news media. And some will be lost to the sands of time. Still, what we know about the hidden world of espionage could fill many volumes.

This book contains a large sampling but still only scratches the surface. The information enclosed covers several eras of history and includes mundane facts, amusing tidbits, and horrifying revelations about clandestine activities of the past. It delves into fictional spies and their creators and describes a few tricks of the trade you might be able to use in a pinch yourself (at your own risk, of course).

Researching this book, I learned that spies are often not rewarded for their work, even if they are on the winning side, that governments always seem to be after each other's technology, and that countries are, as often as not, tricked into war. Also, espionage techniques are routinely used for good, such as thwarting terrorist attacks and rescuing refugees, and, in the US's checkered past, leading enslaved people to freedom. Speaking of which, I also learned that Harriet Tubman was a real-life superhero who should be on all the currency.

Knowledge about the shadowy secret dealings of governments and organizations will make you realize that peace is both precious and fragile. People are often struggling behind the scenes to either keep or break it. We should learn to spot propaganda and misinformation, which has been used too many times to lead us to commit atrocities or enter into war, that most deadly of human pastimes.

In many ways, it would be better if we all stopped this covert battle for power and opted for complete transparency, including sharing technological and scientific discoveries. This would require trust and, looking at past shenanigans, who can blame countries for not trusting each other? But it's up to current and future generations to learn from history (that thing we are told we are doomed to repeat if we don't) and weigh the costs of carrying on the undertaking that is sometimes called "the great game" or "the second oldest profession." I hope you get some of that knowledge from these pages. Then you can make up your own mind on the usefulness of espionage in the modern world.

CHAPTER 1

SPY TRADECRAFT

TECHNIQUES AND TOOLS OF THE TRADE

A: American traitor Benedict Arnold and British agent Joseph Stansbury used a book code to pass information back and forth. The method uses a page number, line number, and word number counted from the left to generate a number that corresponded to a word (the one at that location in a particular book). Both sides have to use the same book. Arnold and Stansbury used *Commentaries on the Laws of England* by Sir William Blackstone. One picked out words from the book to write a message in the numbered code, and the other interpreted the resulting coded message. They also wrote these messages in invisible ink (ink that is invisible until acted upon by a chemical, heat, or something else that renders it visible).

One fictional instance when a book code is used is Graham Greene's *The Human Factor*, where agent Maurice Castle uses a Communist-owned bookstore in London to communicate with his Soviet handler via a book code.

Q: What is the general rule of thumb for assigning an operation's code name?

A: It should be as random as possible, with no connection to the actual work being done on the mission. Some famous missions are:

- **Operation Cornflakes:** Creation and distribution of demoralizing parody postage stamps during WWII.

- **Operation Paperclip:** US recruitment of German rocket scientists.

- **Operation Mincemeat:** Mission by British intelligence during WWII to plant a body disguised as a fictional military captain carrying fake intel to deceive the Germans as to where troops would be landing.

- **Operation Ghost Stories:** The gathering of evidence on a group of Russian sleeper agents masquerading as American suburbanites.

Sometimes agencies or agents pick a name that does tie in with the mission, like "Operation Exodus," which convinced Catholics to flee from North to South Vietnam, but the general rule of thumb is to avoid a name that could lead someone to guess the actual mission.

Q : What is a "dead drop?"

A : A dead drop, also known as a "dead letter box," is a technique where agents and their handlers leave and pick up documents or other items in a prearranged place for exchange so they do not have to meet each other in person. There are agents and handlers who've worked together for years and never met. The location can be any place where something can be concealed without too much danger of the general public stumbling upon it or seeing the operative make the drop or pickup. There's even a specialized hollow contraption called a "dead drop spike" that can be driven into the ground for concealing documents in a waterproof container.

A run-in marker is used in conjunction with a dead drop to signal that a drop has been made. The marker can be anything: an actual mark made with chalk or a marker, a piece of tape or gum, an item left in a certain place in a certain way, or any indicator that the parties have agreed to look out for.

A: A brush pass, also known as "brush contact," is a method of passing information or items while one agent walks past the other. The idea is that the agents will not have a noticeable exchange but look like pedestrians who have just brushed past each other naturally.

The brush pass can involve placing something in the other person's hand, exchanging identical objects, or putting a small item in the other person's pocket, shopping bag, or other place of concealment. Unlike the dead drop, the brush pass method will be less conspicuous if it takes place in a crowd. But it also requires some dexterity.

Q: What does the word "illegals" mean in the context of the espionage world?

A: It is known, and almost expected, that people working as diplomats in a foreign country may be spying on that country. As you'll learn in the pages to come, even Benjamin Franklin acted as a spy during his diplomatic mission to France.

But some spies are sent undercover into another country with no diplomatic ties and without permission to be in the country. These agents are called illegals by people working in intelligence.

Q: What is a "handler" in the spy world?

A: A handler is an intelligence officer tasked with managing agents in the field.

Q: What does "walk-in" mean in espionage parlance?

A: A walk-in is someone from one government who volunteers to spy for another government, often by walking into an embassy (although a potential walk-in can reach out in other ways). Some intelligence officers have said that this is the most common way to get spies from other countries and that trying to recruit people for the task by turning them away from their own government most often fails.

Q: What is a "ghost" in the world of espionage?

A: A ghost is someone who works discreetly to follow and monitor a particular target. This act is sometimes called "ghost surveillance."

Q: What is "pocket litter?"

A: Pocket litter is any item an agent carries around to support their cover story and make it believable. It can include business cards or any other paraphernalia related to whatever business they are supposed to be in, receipts of places they are supposed to have gone, and the like. For example, during the plot to get embassy workers posing as a Canadian film location scouting crew out of Iran, the CIA agent tasked with exfiltrating the group brought various items, including a copy of a trade magazine with an article about the fake film.

Q: What are some high-level categories of intelligence?

A: Intelligence tends to be categorized by its source, and each has a handy abbreviation. If it comes from a human source, it's called HUMINT (human intelligence). If it comes from signals like radio communications, it's called SIGINT (signals intelligence). Two subsets of SIGINT are COMINT (communications intelligence), which is intercepted human communication, and ELINT (electronic intelligence), which is information collected from radar and other systems. If it consists of telemetry signals (say from launched rockets), it's called MASINT (measurement and signature intelligence). Information gathered from images is called IMINT (imagery intelligence). Intel gathered from images and other information specifically about geographical locations is called GEOINT (geospatial intelligence).

Q: What planes were created to keep an eye on possible Russian nuclear sites without risking pilots to anti-aircraft missiles?

A: James Killian (former president of MIT and President Eisenhower's scientific advisor) and Edwin Land (founder of Polaroid) spearheaded a committee of people from academia, the scientific community, and industry to develop a plane that could fly over and photograph the Soviet Union without getting shot down. Richard Bissell, deputy to the CIA's director Allen Dulles, was sent to work with Kelly Johnson at aerospace and defense company Lockheed Martin to develop a plane fitted with high-resolution photographic equipment that could remain low enough to get good photos and high enough to stay out of range of anti-aircraft missiles. They successfully developed the U-2 spy plane.

A: The first electronic satellite that could send and receive information was Sputnik, launched by Russia in 1957.

In 1960, the US launched the Corona satellite, developed by the CIA at their headquarters in Langley, Virginia. It took photographs of Russia and sent the photo negatives down via parachute, which the Air Force had to retrieve from the ocean. It remained active until 1972. You can see one at the National Air and Space Museum in Washington, DC.

In 1976, the KH-11 satellite system was created, the first to transmit digital photographs back to Earth. There are still operational KH-11 satellites.

A US spy satellite called Rhyolite collected and transmitted ELINT and MASINT from Soviet missile test sites in Central Asia to stations in Turkey and Iran before the 1979 Iranian Revolution. At the CIA's Directorate of Science and Technology, created in 1962, experts analyzed these telemetry signals and figured out how to interpret them to learn about the weapons being tested, including their weight, range, accuracy, type of propellant, and warhead yield.

Q: What intelligence specialty is jokingly referred to as "crateology?"

A: Once the US and other countries started gaining high-altitude photographic intelligence from spy planes and spy satellites, they needed experts to interpret them. Enter photo interpreters, who pore over photographs looking for useful information. Among other tasks, they sometimes have to try to determine the contents of shipping crates (i.e., what weapons or vehicles they might contain) by their size and shape—thus, the term "crateology."

Crateology is, of course, not an exact science, but it can come in handy, as it did in 1962 during the Cuban Missile Crisis, when intelligence determined that the Soviets were setting up medium-to intermediate-range ballistic missiles around Cuba.

Q: What vehicle was secretly developed to raise a sunken nuclear submarine?

A: In March 1968, a Soviet nuclear submarine (the K-129) sank in the Pacific Ocean, killing all ninety-eight crewmembers. The Soviets didn't think the US would be able to find it, let alone raise it. But the CIA got to work building the Glomar Explorer, completed in 1974 as part of Project Azorian, to raise the sub. The vehicle even had a cover: a manganese mining exploration vehicle owned by Howard Hughes, who went along with the story and announced he was building such a ship.

The Glomar Explorer included a submersible vehicle with a claw that was used to slowly raise the sub from 17,000 feet down. The submarine broke apart and didn't make it to the surface intact, but US intelligence was able to get useful intel from the 40-foot piece that was recovered, which included two nuclear torpedoes and manuals.

The Glomar Explorer was put to use in oil drilling afterward. It was scrapped in 2015.

Q: What famous early photographer and inventor of the mug shot also spied for the Union?

A: Alexander Gardner was a journalist from Scotland who emigrated to the United States in the 1850s. In search of a career change, he got a job in New York working with photographer Mathew Brady. During the Civil War, Gardner used his photographic equipment (including a mobile darkroom) to act as a photojournalist (America's first) and document the war with photographs.

But he also used his camera to spy for the Union, taking pictures of documents, Confederate soldiers, battle sites, and other things that might be of use to the North, and sharing them with Union officers. He also reportedly photographed both Lincoln (many times) and John Wilkes Booth, before the actor turned presidential assassin.

After the war, he came up with the concept of the mug shot for the Washington Police Department.

Sadly, many of the negatives were destroyed a couple of decades after his death. A scrap dealer reportedly bought a large cache of glass negatives, scraped off the images, and sold the glass.

Q: What nonhuman animals have been enlisted to do spy work?

A: Horses have carried riders bearing secret messages since the dawn of civilization, but other animals have been drafted into service as intelligence operators. Or even bombs.

Carrier pigeons are known as message carriers. A famous WWI hero was Cher Ami, a pigeon who carried a message from surrounded American soldiers and made it to his destination even after being shot in the leg and breast. Soldiers made him a wooden leg, but he died the next year of his injuries.

People have also been known to strap cameras to pigeons and use them as drones. The British had a division they called the Special Pigeon Service.

The Office of Strategic Services (OSS) tried to attack Japan with bats during World War II. The bats were wearing backpacks with incendiary devices, and the hope was that they would burn down whatever structures they settled in. Instead, they set the base where they were being tested on fire.

In a sad instance of animal experimentation in the 1960s, the CIA had a program called Acoustic Kitty. They surgically implanted batteries and a listening device into a cat and trained it to follow instructions so that they could control where it went (supposedly). On its first mission, the cat was released, walked into the street, and got hit by a taxicab.

Q: What is the distinction between intelligence and counter-intelligence work?

A: Intelligence is the work of gathering, intercepting, or decoding information from foreign countries or whatever entity is considered a rival. Counterintelligence is the work of thwarting foreign agents from being able to do the same.

Q: What is a double agent?

A: A double agent pretends to spy for one entity while really working for another.

Q: What is a mole?

A: A mole is a foreign agent who penetrates an intelligence agency and pretends to work for that agency when really acting for and reporting to a foreign agency or entity. A mole is a more specific sort of double agent.

Q: What is a honey pot?

A: Also known as a honey trap, a honey pot is an operation whereby an agent is seduced and blackmailed or otherwise entrapped with sex by a foreign operative.

Q: What is a burn notice?

A: As ominous as it sounds, the "burn" in burn notice refers to burning documents. If a spy is found to be unreliable, a burn notice is issued and all reports from that spy are destroyed (plus, presumably, the spy is no longer used).

CHAPTER 2

EVERYDAY ESPIONAGE

TIPS, TRICKS, AND DANGERS

A : We live in what some call a "post-truth society." What is one to do when they suspect someone of lying? There are signs that may indicate when someone is not being truthful, but none are foolproof.

It helps to know a little about a person's behavior under normal circumstances (i.e., when they aren't lying) to interpret whether what you think is a sign is just how they normally act. If you want to confront someone about a potential lie but don't already know them, you can try to make them comfortable (be nice, have them sit in a comfy spot, and ask them if they want anything to drink, for instance). Then you can ask them simple questions you don't think they would lie about and observe their physical and vocal reactions and mannerisms.

A sign of a lie in one person might not be the case in another. People have idiosyncrasies. But some experts suggest that showing multiple red flags is a good indicator someone is lying.

Some verbal signs include the following: not answering a question directly, hesitating to answer, saying the question back, using formal or qualifying language, providing very little detail or giving too much extraneous detail, stammering or rambling, overreacting to a question, and changing vocal tone, pitch, or tempo.

Some physical signs include the following: freezing like a deer in headlights, shifting or pointing their feet toward the nearest exit (as if they want to escape), putting physical barriers between themselves and the questioner, shaking their head when saying something positive or nodding when saying something negative, changing their blinking rate, smiling a fake smile, staring at the questioner too intently, or avoiding eye contact. There is also something called "duping delight," when someone smiles unexpectedly while talking about something serious.

Under certain circumstances, a person innocent of an infraction tends to suggest a strict punishment for that crime, while a person guilty of that infraction tends to suggest leniency for it.

On the flip side, if you need to lie for safety reasons, the above becomes a list of what to try not to do. It will be difficult in a tense situation or if you have no acting skills, but at least try to stay calm and act natural.

If you find yourself on the other end of a polygraph ("lie detector") machine, there are techniques for beating them based on the fact that they don't so much measure lies as they do anxiety. Experts suggest trying to stay calm, controlling your breathing, pausing before answering. Think of something that would make you anxious (and clench your butt cheeks together) when telling the truth, and think of something calming if you are lying, to throw off the tester's results. Polygraphs are not considered terribly reliable. If you have a choice, don't submit to one.

Q: How do you free your hands from duct tape or zip ties?

A: Duct tape is the easiest constraint from which to break free, but if your hands are bound in front of you, the same technique may work for both duct tape and zip ties. While your wrists are being duct taped or zip tied, if possible, lean forward, hold your arms out in front of you as far as you can, and press your forearms together all the way from your hands to your elbows. When the coast is clear, to escape the duct tape, raise your arms as high as possible above your head, then quickly swing them down and out to the sides past your hips. In the case of zip ties, first use your teeth to rotate the zip tie lock to the top center (where your hands or wrists meet), then perform the same arm swing as with duct tape, but with more force.

There is a possibility it won't work. (There's also a good chance it will hurt, especially with the zip ties. You have to weigh the risk versus the danger of not trying). If the duct tape doesn't break or you can't make the motion for whatever reason, find any solid object with a 90-degree angle, put the tape where your wrists meet at the edge, and run the tape back and forth until it tears and breaks. Once your hands are free, you can use them to remove any other bindings.

One possible alternate method for zip ties that won't break requires having several feet of paracord (nylon parachute cord) on you. Some shoelaces are made of this material. You can use paracord to saw through a zip tie, but you need to be able to pull it back and forth over the zip tie (tricky without your hands free). If you have enough paracord, you can put the halfway mark of the cord on the zip tie and drape it over both sides, then make loops for your feet on either end of the cord, put your feet in the loops, lie back, and pedal your feet as if you are riding a bike until the cord saws through the plastic.

Q: How might you escape from rope?

A: The escape method for rope differs from that of duct tape or zip ties. First, instead of keeping your hands and arms together, you want to try to keep your hands together but your elbows apart when someone is tying your hands with rope. Then, when your attacker isn't looking, put your palms together, stretch your arms out in front of you, and move them back and forth in opposite directions from each other until you free one of your hands.

If that doesn't work and you have paracord on you, put the halfway mark of the cord on the rope and drape it over both sides. Make loops for your feet on either end of the cord, put your feet in the loops, lie back, and pedal your feet as if you are riding a bike until the cord saws through the rope.

Q : How do you escape from a locked trunk?

A : The trunks of most modern cars have an escape lever, possibly glow-in-the-dark. In that case, just find and pull that lever. In an older car, get on your hands and knees and try pushing upward with your back until it opens. If that doesn't work, try kicking the back of the back seat until it folds down, and crawl out that way, although that could be more perilous if your kidnapper is still in the car.

Q: How can you detect or thwart listening devices and hidden cameras?

A: You don't need special equipment for your initial scan. If you are checking a room you frequent, visually scan for anything that's changed and take a closer look if you detect anything. Also, inspect anything that is plugged in to check for new non-battery-powered devices. If you have a radio going, you can turn the dial and listen for distortions, which might indicate a bug.

You can also hop on your computer and check to see what devices are connected to your Wi-Fi router. Any new device listed could be a bug or other connected surveillance device. And a new network could be a new device's own hot spot.

If you are worried about cameras, simply shining a light around and looking for reflections off a lens is a nice, low-tech visual scan. There are even phone apps specifically designed for this purpose. To look for night-vision cameras, you might need an infrared scanner.

If you have a radio frequency detector, you can turn off all smart devices that connect to your Wi-Fi and walk around scanning for signals. You can also get devices that scan for laser beams and radio waves. Another device called a nonlinear junction detector can detect anything with a semiconductor (but they cost in the thousands or tens of thousands).

Back to phones, phone apps exist that make either mild or inaudible noise that interferes with listening equipment. You can also buy a bug jammer or a bug detector that can both detect and block transmissions.

Alternatively, if you don't want to bother with any of this but still want to thwart any would-be listeners, you can mask the conversation with music or other noise, or go have your talk in a noisy outdoor spot (near traffic, a construction site, or a rushing river). That is, if it's not too loud to hear each other.

Q: How can you stop someone from stealing data from your credit cards and keycards?

A: Skimmers, or data-grabbers, allow someone to read the data on your access cards, credit cards, and even your phone, if they get within close enough proximity. If you can't just leave them at home, you can buy a pouch, wallet, purse, or other carrying case that blocks radio-frequency identification signals. They are quite common and inexpensive these days. Or, if you don't want to spend much money, you can wrap whatever you want to protect in aluminum foil.

Q: How can you throw together a disguise?

A: To look like a different person, you can change your hairstyle, cut, or color. If you have facial hair, growing it out or shaving it into a goatee or other style you don't normally wear can make you look quite different. You can also try hair extensions, wigs, and fake facial hair.

Wear glasses if you don't already wear them, and switch to contacts if you do. Specialty contacts can even change the color of your eyes. Makeup can also alter your appearance drastically and quickly.

Try clothes that you don't normally wear, but that won't stand out in the environment you'll be walking around in. Bland is better than eye-catching if you're trying to go unnoticed. Also, hide any distinguishing features like moles or tattoos. Or, alternately, add a fake mole or temporary tattoo.

To alter your appearance quickly, you can also give changing your mannerisms a try. Improve your posture if you normally slouch, and vice versa. For the much longer disguise game, gaining or losing weight definitely changes your appearance.

If you are putting on a disguise to go along with a cover story, be sure to have pocket litter. If you are posing as a journalist, for example, that might be a small notepad and pen, a recording device, and some sort of press credentials.

Don't pick something you can't pull off, like rocket scientist if you don't know a thing about physics or math. And if you are really going to try to pull off another profession or persona, you might want to get some acting lessons, or at least practice.

Q: How do you protect your personal data from hackers?

A: The first line of defense is antivirus software. Make sure you have software from a legitimate company, and update it frequently. You can set it to automatically install updates.

But an attack via a forced break-in is not the only way the bad guys can access your computer. One major way evildoers get access to computers and computer networks is via social engineering, which means they trick people into letting them in. They might send phishing emails that look legitimate and that ask you to click a link or enter personal data. A link might, in turn, take you to a site that looks legitimate but is really a fake setup to harvest your login credentials or install malware on your computer or phone. Spear phishing is a more targeted attack where the sender knows something about you (where you work, companies you do business with) and crafts the email to really look and sound like it's from some entity you have a connection to.

If there is any doubt, don't click on any email links. In most cases, you can go directly to the site that the email appears to be from. Another rule of thumb is never to divulge user IDs, passwords, account numbers, or anything else that could be used to get into an account, system, or computer you have access to. For the most part, no one ever needs to know your passwords to anything, and if they ask for them, that's a huge red flag. Another red flag is hearing them say anything to try to scare you into responding, like claiming your email account will be deleted unless you enter the password or that money is being withdrawn from an account.

Even if you are cautious, someone else on the same network might not be, which could compromise everyone's data in a network. So safeguard your own data and passwords, keep as much personal data off your work computer as possible, and use two-part authentication whenever you can (which requires some other authentication on top of username and password, like a number sent to your phone via text or a code generated by an app).

And data theft isn't all about remote methods. Some attacks happen in person. To keep someone from just walking up and accessing your computer, turn on password protection and lock your screen anytime you leave your desk. There is usually a quick key combination for this.

As people do more and more on the cloud, it's not just your hardware that needs to be safeguarded. If someone has enough information about you, they may be able to call a company you have an account with and provide enough personal details to trick them into providing access. People put out a lot of information about themselves on social media. Have you ever seen a post asking you to build your motto or your post-apocalyptic name or any other silly phrase by picking a word or phrase that corresponds with your birth month and birthday? If you respond, you've given someone at least part of your birthday. Be mindful of the information you share online.

Another method of tricking people into allowing access to a device is the fake Wi-Fi hub. If you see a Wi-Fi network called "airport" when you are at the airport, it might actually be a guy sitting nearby who has created a hot spot and is ready to harvest whatever he can from people who connect to it.

Some ne'er-do-wells install malware on flash drives and leave them out for some unwitting person to plug into their computer's USB port. Once plugged in, the malware installs, so leave stray thumb drives alone.

The lowest tech form of spying on your computer is just viewing what's on your screen up close or from a distance with a long-range camera or binoculars. So try to sit with your back to a wall, or purchase a polarized screen shield that makes it so that the screen can only be viewed from one angle. If your screen faces a window, close the blinds. And, once again, lock your screen when you leave your desk. Or carry your laptop with you.

CHAPTER 3

THAT'S ANCIENT HISTORY

EARLY HISTORICAL AND MYTHOLOGICAL ESPIONAGE

A : Until someone makes an even more ancient discovery, the earliest known reference to spying is on a clay tablet dated around 1800 BCE (nearly four thousand years ago), from ancient Mesopotamia. In 1933, after locals digging a grave discovered an ancient statue in Tell Hariri, Syria, near the west bank of the Euphrates River, the Louvre Museum in Paris sent André Parrot, curator for the Department of Near Eastern Antiquities—and decades later director of the Louvre—with a crew to begin excavation. Very early in the dig, the archaeologists discovered another statue, this one labeled in cuneiform as a likeness of King Lamgi-Mari, ruler of the ancient city of Mari.

The dig went on from 1933 to 1939, when the archeologists unearthed many artifacts, including a huge palace spanning about 10 acres. They found over 24,000 clay tablets inscribed in cuneiform within the palace. The tablets were translated by Assyriologists in Paris over years.

The tablets revealed tremendous insights on the inner workings of the Mari government, from a mail system used for sending and receiving clay tablets to posts in the desert to watch for encroachment by neighboring nomadic tribes. One of the tablets contained a message to the king from an officer named Bannum, reporting that all the Benjamite villages were sending each other fire signals (the fastest form of communication in the area at the time). The message stated that the officer would investigate what they meant, that the guard should be strengthened, and that the king should remain inside the palace.

Mari likely withstood whatever the Benjamites were planning at that time, but Babylonian King Hammurabi took over and partially destroyed the city in 1761 BCE. Still, much of the palace remained intact after this attack despite an obvious attempt to burn it.

Sadly, the area was occupied by the Islamic State of Iraq and al-Sham (ISIS) in 2014, and recent photographs show that the site has been decimated both by looters digging for antiquities and possible aerial bombing.

A : Don't look a gift horse in the mouth, unless that horse is made of wood. In Greek mythology and epic poetry, Paris, a prince of Troy, ran away with Helen, said to be the most beautiful woman in the world. She is also called "the face that launched a thousand ships." Her husband, King Menelaus of Sparta, was none too happy about losing his wife and retaliated. Greek armies besieged the thick-walled city of Troy in an attempt to get Helen back, but they had no luck for an entire decade.

Per the Roman poet Virgil, the battle-weary Greeks came up with a clever covert operation. They constructed a large wooden horse, left it at the gates of the city, and set sail, but only to the nearby isle of Tenedos. The Trojans thought the Greeks were sailing for Greece and, having been cooped up for a long while, opened the gates, looked around, and found the horse at the Greek camp.

Some Trojans, including Capys and Laocoön, argued against bringing the artificial beast inside, fearing it was a trick. Laocoön even threw a spear and pierced the horse, causing the Greeks within to groan, but the sound was drowned out by the shouts of Trojans, who had found and captured a lone Greek named Sinon. Sinon told the Trojans that if they wanted to satisfy their thirst for revenge, they could strike him down. But he wove a tale that Ulysses had a grudge against him and that the Greeks had sacrificed him so that the gods would calm the weather enough for them to make it home. Sinon said that he was chosen as the sacrifice because of the grudge, but he'd escaped and hidden, and the Greek armies had sailed away. One might call his tale a cover story.

King Priam told Sinon not to fear and that Troy would take him in. When the king asked about the horse, Sinon claimed that it was built to appease the goddess Minerva, because Greek soldiers had slain her temple's guardians and stolen her statue. If they brought it into Troy and didn't damage it, the Greeks' good fortune would be overturned and transferred to the Trojans. They bought his story and hoisted the horse over the city walls and into the city. Cassandra, daughter of Priam, foretold what was to come, but no one believed her (such was the nature of her curse from the god Apollo for refusing his advances).

That night, the Greeks sailed back from Tenedos, and Sinon unlocked the horse and let out its concealed passengers. Greek soldiers exited its hollow belly and opened the city gates to let the rest of their army in. Troy fell, and the ill-meant gift is referred to as the Trojan Horse.

These days, computer malware that hides in seemingly innocuous code is named after the Trojan Horse, as is anyone or anything that hides its true purpose.

As to the mythological nature of the Trojan War and the city itself, some people believe that a buried city found in Turkey around 1870 is the actual city of Troy. An archeologist from Germany, Heinrich Schliemann, unearthed 82 feet of ruins later found to be nine cities stacked on top of each other. One of the cities had very thick walls (just as Troy was purported to have) and had been destroyed around 1180 BCE. No one knows its identity for sure, but it is possible that it is the city that inspired Homer's *Iliad*, about the siege and fall of Troy, which inspired later stories like Virgil's poem *The Aeneid*.

Q: What ancient civilization used spies to thwart serf revolts?

A: The government of Sparta assumed ownership of an entire caste of people called helots. They were not official citizens of Sparta, but they were enlisted to fight alongside Spartan soldiers in wars and had more freedom than a typical slave in other parts of Greece at the time. Many were of Messenian or Laconian origin.

Sparta was wary of revolts by the helots, who far outnumbered the citizens of Sparta. The city took measures to prevent such an occurrence, including creating its own secret police force to keep an eye on the helots and discover any attempts at revolt. Despite these tactics, or maybe even because of them, two notable helot revolts took place: one after Sparta was decimated by an earthquake in the 460s BCE, and another led by a demoted Spartan named Cinadon around 398 BCE.

Thucydides tells of an event after the end of hostilities between Sparta and Athens in the 420s BCE (although historians don't know if the story is true). Spartan leaders asked the helots to put forth two thousand of their rank that had performed the most distinguished service to Sparta during the war, with hints that they would be rewarded with freedom. Two thousand helots presented themselves, and, thinking they were now free, celebrated by putting garlands on their heads and walking in procession around the temples. But instead of being allowed to enjoy freedom, they were put to death. The idea was that this group contained the people most likely to start a revolt.

Sparta also held an annual ritual when they declared war on the helots and sent their young soldiers-in-training out to kill some of them. Historians are not sure how long this tradition persisted, but it's no wonder Sparta feared that this put-upon group might rebel at any moment.

Q: What biblical character accused his brothers of being spies as part of an elaborate trick to reunite with his family?

A: In the book of Genesis, Joseph, son of Jacob (also referred to as Israel), was sold into slavery by ten of his eleven brothers. They were jealous that their father loved him the most, as evidenced by the many-colored coat their father made Joseph. They were also upset after Joseph told them of two dreams in which he ended up in power over them. The brothers tricked their father into believing Joseph was dead by presenting the coat to him with goat's blood on it.

His new owners brought Joseph to Egypt, where he eventually rose up to be the Pharaoh's right-hand man after successfully interpreting one of the Pharaoh's dreams to mean that Egypt would have seven years of plenty followed by seven years of famine. The Pharaoh renamed Joseph Zaphenath-Paneah.

Many years later, when Joseph's family suffered from Canaan's famine, they sent all but his youngest brother into Egypt with money to buy grain. They were brought to Joseph (under his new name), who recognized them as his brothers, but they no longer recognized him. He accused them of being spies, which they protested. Joseph held them for three days, ordered them to bring their younger brother as proof that they were truthful, and sent all but one (Simeon) away with the grain and (unbeknownst to the brothers until they returned home) the money.

When the family finished the grain, the brothers returned with twice the money, presents, and their younger brother Benjamin. Joseph sent them away again with grain and their money, and had his servant hide a silver cup in Benjamin's bag. Joseph then ordered the servant to accuse them of stealing the cup and bring them back. At that time, Joseph said whomever was found with the cup would become his servant.

But when the brothers begged him not to take their brother, he broke down and admitted who he was and said he bore them no grudge for what they did to him because it led him to his current position. He sent them back with riches, food, and wagons to bring the family to Egypt. The father reunited with his lost son, who settled the whole family in Goshen.

The stage and screen musical *Joseph and the Amazing Technicolor Dreamcoat* by Andrew Lloyd Webber and Tim Rice is based on this story.

Q : What biblical figure sent scouts into Canaan to report back on the area?

A : In the Bible's book of Numbers, Moses, at the behest of God, sent a leader from each tribe (a dozen in all) from the wilderness (desert) of Paran into Canaan to surveil the area, report back on the condition of the land, the cities, and the people, and bring back the "fruit of the land."

They came back forty days later, and Joshua and Caleb reported that the land was fruitful (and brought produce to prove it), but the rest of the scouts reported that the people were strong and the cities were walled. They expressed misgivings about trying to take over and settle there. Save Moses, his brother (and priest of the Israelites) Aaron, Joshua, and Caleb, the people of the tribes of Reuben, Simeon, Judah, Issachar, Zebulun, Gad, Asher, Dan, Naphtali, Benjamin, Manasseh, and Ephraim were afraid to try to conquer the people of Canaan and wailed about their situation.

It angered God that the people didn't believe his signs, and he threatened to smite them. Moses talked him out of smiting everyone, but God told him to let his people know that every one of them who was 20 or older and had spoken against his plan would die in the wilderness, and their children would wander for forty years before they would be able to settle in the promised land.

A: The book of Joshua states that after the death of Moses, God bade Joshua to take the people to the promised land. Joshua sent two spies from Shittim into Jericho. They stayed at the home of Rahab (a prostitute), who hid them on her roof among the flax, and when the king of Jericho's men came to her searching for the spies, she claimed they had already left.

Rahab's house was propped against the town wall, so she was able to help them down the other side with a rope. She suggested they hide in the mountain for three days to evade the king's men, and she asked the spies to return her kindness by promising to spare her entire family when their people took Jericho. They told her to bring her whole family into her house and bind the window they were just let out of with a scarlet cord as a signal.

The spies hid in the mountains as instructed and later made it back to Joshua. He led the Israelites to Jordan. There, the waters dried up as the priests carried over the Ark of the Covenant (the vessel containing the Ten Commandments), allowing the people to pass through to Gilgal near Jericho.

At Jericho, seven priests blowing ram's horns, priests carrying the ark, and armed men circled the wall of the city once a day for six days, and seven times on the seventh day. The people shouted along with the horns on the seventh turn, and the walls of Jericho miraculously fell. They took the town easily, killing everyone except Rahab and her family.

Q : What biblical femme fatale learned the secret of Samson's strength?

A : In the book of Judges, Samson was blessed with such great strength that no one could defeat him. Two women betrayed him, but the second was the more egregious (and famous) instance.

The first was his Philistine bride. At their wedding feast, he bet a group of guests that they couldn't guess his riddle. If they could, he'd give them thirty sheets and thirty changes of clothing. If they couldn't, they'd give the same to him, and they agreed. The riddle was: "Out of the eater came forth meat, and out of the strong came forth sweetness." The Philistines couldn't possibly have guessed, because it had to do with something only Samson knew about (Samson had torn a lion in half, and the next time he saw the carcass, a honeycomb was within it.)

The Philistine feasters threatened to burn the house of the new bride's father if she didn't find out the answer and tell them. She asked Samson and wept until he told her. The guests were able to give him the riddle's answer, so he knew that she had disclosed it. He killed the men and left his wife at her father's. He eventually came back to retrieve her, but her father, thinking that he had abandoned her, had given her to one of Samson's friends.

In anger, Samson burned the Philistines' fields. The Philistines, in turn, burned his wife and her father to death. So Samson killed more of them. The Philistines sent the men of Judah to bind Samson and hand him over to them. Samson agreed to go with them, but when he got there, he easily broke his bonds, picked up the jawbone of an ass, and slew one thousand more Philistines. During another attempt on his life, this one at Gaza, he escaped and walked away with the city's gate.

There seemed to be no stopping him, until he fell for the femme fatale Delilah, his second betrayer. The Philistine leaders, still looking to kill Samson, convinced Delilah to find out what made Samson so strong by promising her 1,100 pieces of silver from each of them. She asked Samson every day, and he lied to her every day by telling her a different method for taking his strength. She would try the method each time and discover that he had lied and could easily break free.

She finally wore him down, and he admitted that if his locks were shaved, he would lose his strength. When he fell asleep, she had his hair shaved, and the Philistines were able to poke out his eyes, then gather to celebrate. He avenged himself by praying for strength just one more time and pulling on the pillars that held up the house where they were celebrating, causing the house to collapse and killing himself and the Philistines who'd captured him.

So his first love was threatened into spying and his second bribed into it, two common methods of spy recruitment.

Q: What biblical figure's name is synonymous with the word "traitor?"

A: Several books of the Bible (the Gospels of Matthew, Mark, Luke, and John) tell the story of Judas Iscariot's betrayal of Jesus Christ. He was one of Jesus' twelve apostles and the treasurer. The head priest Caiaphas, the other chief priests, and the scribes and elders of the church wanted to stop Jesus. Judas went to the chief priests and asked them what they'd give him for betraying Jesus to them, and they offered thirty pieces of silver.

Jesus and his disciples went to Gethsemane. Judas came with armed men, who were told that the person Judas kissed would be Jesus. Judas kissed Jesus, and the men took him. The chief priests convinced people to bear false witness against Jesus, but none of their stories agreed. So the high priest asked Jesus if he was the son of God, and when he said yes, charged him with blasphemy and sentenced him to death—a sentence carried out by the governor, Pontius Pilate, via crucifixion.

Judas repented, went to the temple, threw the thirty pieces of silver to the floor in front of the priests, and went off and killed himself. To this day, to call someone a Judas is to label them a traitor.

Q: What ancient Sanskrit text details official uses of spying in governance?

A: Kautilya's *Arthashastra*, an ancient Indian text written in Sanskrit around 300 BCE, deals with governing and includes several potential uses for spies. Ruses, for instance, can test the loyalty or purity of government ministers. In one ruse, a priest, commanding soldier, or another minister is seemingly fired, then approaches other ministers to see if they are willing to overthrow the king. Another ruse, called a love allurement (today called a honey pot), involves sending a woman from the king's harem to entice ministers by offering wealth and pretending that the queen wants them in her chambers.

The text recommends those who passed certain tests be assigned to roles related to those tests (e.g., if they were tested with wealth and passed, they were to work in revenue, or if they were tested with sex and passed, they might be put in charge of the pleasure grounds). Interestingly, the book calls for the ministers who failed tests to be relegated to jobs in timber, mining, and manufacturing.

The *Arthashastra* also has a chapter on setting up networks of spies under various covers, like merchants, mendicants, colleagues, classmates, farmers, and landlords, among others, to gather intelligence related to crimes and other wrongdoing. It required that their claims be corroborated by two others (three sources in total). It even spells out using counterintelligence agents to thwart the actions of foreign spies.

The book speaks of institutes of espionage and mentions the spies and officers of the institutes not knowing each other (i.e., never meeting, which is a bit of spy tradecraft still practiced in some situations so that one spy getting caught doesn't lead back to another agent or a whole spy ring).

Q: Which king showed outside spies around his army camps to show the enemy his might?

A: Herodotus wrote a story of King Xerxes of Persia and his treatment of three Greek spies sent to Sardis, a prominent city within the Persian empire. These spies were tasked with scoping out the king's military might. The generals caught and questioned them, then sentenced them to die. When Xerxes heard, he sent some of his spearmen to bring him the spies.

The spies were brought before Xerxes and told him of their purpose. Instead of having them killed, Xerxes had the spearmen show them around his armies and then let them go. He explained that if they killed the three soldiers, that wouldn't do much damage to the Greek armies, but if the soldiers let their leaders know how strong Xerxes's forces were, they might just surrender (an act of psychological warfare and using another group's spies against them).

Q: What ancient Asian empire hired Europeans to gather intel?

A: Genghis Khan (or Chenggis Khan, originally named Temüjin) united Mongolia. He and his offspring expanded their empire over multiple continents. Genghis Khan also instituted a policy of diplomatic immunity.

The Mongols wisely gathered intelligence on areas before invading them, but they knew Mongolian spies would stand out beyond Asia. So they hired Europeans to spy in European areas.

Q: Which Chinese general wrote of the importance of spying in warfare?

A: Around 490 BCE, Chinese general Sun Tzu wrote *The Art of War*, a work still in wide circulation today. In it, he frequently refers to espionage in warfare, both in regard to using spies and safeguarding against the enemy's spies. Early in the book, he states, "All warfare is based on deception." He devoted the entire final chapter to the use of spies. He touts the virtues of foreknowledge and encourages paying spies to find out the condition of the enemy because warfare without foreknowledge is much more costly.

Sun Tzu suggests employing five different types of spies: "local" spies (inhabitants of the enemy's area), "inward" spies (officials of the enemy), "converted" spies (captured spies converted into double agents), "doomed" spies (spies sent out to get noticed by the enemy to spread false information), and "surviving" spies (spies who bring intel from the enemy's camp). He suggests killing spies who divulge secrets, along with the person to whom they told the secret. But he also suggests rewarding spies, even an enemy's captured spies, who should be well treated in order to convert them.

A : Julius Caesar, general and, later, emperor of Rome, mentions his use of spies several times in his autobiographical tome *The Gallic Wars*, about his military exploits in Gaul in the 50s BCE. Caesar would send scouts to check on the condition or location of enemy forces (or sometimes allied forces) and scope out the lay of the land to decide on the best travel routes and find suitable areas for his army to camp. He even mentions the existence of a spy sloop (boat), presumably for reconnaissance by water.

His work also mentions his enemies' uses of scouts. At one point, when the Romans were trying to attack Avaricum, Vercingetorix (one of the Gallic leaders) reportedly camped fifteen miles away from the town in the woods and sent trusted scouts every hour to report on what was going on at Avaricum. He would then act based on their intelligence. He also kept watch on the Roman army's food-gathering expeditions and attacked the forces when they got too scattered. However the skirmishes went, Caesar ultimately won the war.

A: Two merchants from Venice, Buono da Malamocco and Rustico da Torcello, pilfered the purported remains of Saint Mark from the city of Alexandria, Egypt, around 828 ACE. Venice considered Saint Mark their patron saint and wished to "repatriate" him to their city to attract religious tourists. The merchants reportedly took the remains of Saint Mark and replaced them with those of Saint Claudia to hide the act, with the help of monks who supposedly feared the church might be pillaged by the governor of Alexandria for its marble.

The merchants put Saint Mark's body in a basket filled with cabbage and pork, the latter so that Muslim guards wouldn't search the container, and sailed it back to Venice, where the Basilica di San Marco (St. Mark's Basilica) was built to entomb it.

One British historian, Andrew Chugg, believes that the body the merchants stole wasn't that of Saint Mark, but was instead that of Alexander the Great, whose body disappeared sometime during the fourth century. According to him, Saint Mark's body appeared around the time Alexander's disappeared, and he cited some early Christian sources that say Saint Mark was cremated. He conjectured that someone may have disguised Alexander's body as Saint Mark to protect it from rebelling Christians and argued that it should be exhumed and given a DNA test.

Q: What group of stealth killers got their nickname from a drug?

A: The group who came to be known as the Assassins were the Nizari Ismailis, a sect of Shiite Muslims in an area now known as Syria and Iran. They captured the mountain castle at Alamut in Syria around 1090, along with a few others in the area. Due to their small numbers, they practiced guerilla warfare, espionage, and, as the nickname would suggest, assassination of their enemies (including rival leaders and crusaders from Europe).

Legends that came back from crusaders and other travelers to the area painted these Assassins as stealthy murder aficionados who were trained from a young age and brainwashed by their leader, the Old Man of the Mountain (Aloadin), into loyalty through drugs and a paradise-like habitation. The word "assassin" comes from these legends, which prompted outsiders to call them hashishins (or hashish eaters).

Although the more outlandish of the stories were likely apocryphal, the group really did have a leader referred to as the Old Man of the Mountain: Rashid al-Din Sinan, who ruled in the twelfth century.

The Mongols overtook the Nizari Ismailis around 1256.

Q: What fighting style known for stealth originated with peasants resisting warlords?

A: From around 1494 to the 1580s, the Japanese province of Iga was an independent area that managed to withstand takeover from the outside. When they were finally ransacked by warlords, the peasantry developed fighting techniques to resist the usurpers. This style evolved into ninjutsu, and the practitioners were called ninja. The ninja were known to fight with stealth, speed, and unique weapons like *shuriken* (throwing stars), *tekko-kagi* (claws), and *tekagi* (hooks for climbing). They are also known for their head-to-toe black outfits that hide their identities (and in the dark, their presence).

Ninja have been mythologized into almost preternaturally stealthy assassins, and Iga locals created a sort of propaganda, replete with false documents, about the ninja to make it appear that they'd existed much longer than they actually had. Rulers from other regions in Japan later hired ninjas for protection and spy work.

The mythologized ninja appear regularly in comics, movies, and other pop culture entertainment. But it was a real group of people, and two heads of ancient ninja clans are reportedly still around. Jinichi Kawakami, head of the Ban family from the Koka ninja clan, is acknowledged by the Ninja Museum of Iga-ryu as the last grandmaster. Another practitioner, Masaaki Hatsumi, claims to be the grandmaster of the Togakure ninja clan.

Kawakami teaches ninja history at Mie University, and Hatsumi is the founder of the Bujinkan school of martial arts. Both say they will not name a successor as grandmaster.

CHAPTER 4

ROYAL INTRIGUE AND HOLY SPIES

Q: What story of the rescue of a captive king may have been planted to hide the court's intelligence-gathering methods?

A: On the way home from the Third Crusade, Richard I of England (aka Richard the Lionheart) had to land at Venice due to bad weather. There, he was captured by Austrian Duke Leopold. Leopold imprisoned him at Dürnstein Castle, then transferred him to German emperor Henry VI. The emperor demanded a humongous sum (a king's ransom) of 150,000 marks, reportedly nearly three times the royal Crown's annual revenue, and which England raised mainly through the machinations of Richard's mother, Eleanor of Aquitaine, via selling off lands and valuables and heavily taxing the populace. The legend of Robin Hood may have been inspired by this period of high taxation. The ransom was paid, and Richard was released and returned to a financially strapped England.

Legend has it that a French troubadour named Blondel and Richard I had written a song together that no one else knew. When Richard went missing, Blondel went searching for him. At every castle he visited, he sang the first verse of the song. When he reached Dürnstein Castle and sang, the king sang the next verse from the tower and was discovered.

But England knew where he was. One scholar thinks that the Blondel story might have been spread by the English so that people wouldn't guess at their sources.

Q: Which famous lover moonlighted as a spy?

A: Giacomo Casanova (aka Chevalier de Seingalt) was born in Venice, Italy, in 1725. He is best known for bedding a great many women. He is so famous for this, in fact, that the word "Casanova" now means a man who gets around in that regard.

But the great lover also made a living as a con man and spy. After escaping imprisonment in Venice (for being a magician), he went to Paris, where the French foreign minister hired him to gather intelligence on the British fleet that was docked at Dunkirk during the Seven Years' War between France and Great Britain. He managed to hobnob with British officers, and his mission was a success.

He bounced all over Europe, occasionally fleeing creditors. In 1763, he attempted to sell Venice an industrial secret for dying cloth red, but they didn't take him up on it. In 1774, he did, however, end up working as a spy for the Venetian State Inquisitors, with which he had been in trouble before, but which thankfully wasn't as deadly as the best-known inquisitorial body, the Tribunal of the Holy Office of the Inquisition (aka the Spanish Inquisition).

In 1785, he became the librarian for Count von Waldstein in Bohemia. Casanova died in 1798. Memoirs of his exploits were published after his death.

Q: Who ran the first official royal spy ring in England?

A: A rift between Protestants and Catholics in England began around 1533 when Henry VIII wanted a divorce, forbidden under Catholicism. When he couldn't get permission from the Catholic church, he created the Protestant Church of England (also referred to as the Anglican Church), with himself as head, and started disbanding the monasteries. His son and young successor, King Edward VI, continued disbanding monasteries in England. When Edward died at fifteen, his sister Mary Tudor, who was still a Catholic, took the throne and began putting Protestants to death for heresy, earning her the nickname "Bloody Mary."

Mary's half-sister Elizabeth I succeeded her. A Protestant who made Catholic mass illegal (again), Elizabeth instituted fines for people who didn't attend the Church of England. In 1570, Pope Pius V excommunicated Elizabeth from the Catholic church via the papal bull "Regnans in Excelsis," which said her Catholic subjects should try to depose her. Elizabeth banned priests from England, made sheltering them an act of treason, and had many who came to England put to death. Catholics had to worship underground and priests had to go into hiding. France and Spain, Catholic countries, were recurring adversaries of England.

Sir Francis Walsingham was a Protestant who studied law at Cambridge. He lived in Italy during the reign of Bloody Mary, but returned and became Elizabeth I's ambassador to France in 1570. In 1573, she made him secretary of state and a privy council member.

Walsingham created a spy ring for Queen Elizabeth I, consisting of people from various walks of life, including merchants, sailors, and writers, which he used to gather intelligence about potential plots to overthrow Elizabeth (particularly by the Catholic Mary

Queen of Scots, aka Mary Stuart) and possible plots of Spain and France against England. He also kept a group of codebreakers working to decrypt any secret messages his ring intercepted.

His surveillance bore fruit. He caught wind of a courier between Mary, Queen of Scots and the country of France, named Francis Throckmorton. Walsingham had Throckmorton watched and eventually arrested. Under torture, Throckmorton confessed that he was part of a plan to help Spain and France invade England, and he gave up his coconspirators. Throckmorton was executed (via hanging, drawing, and quartering). But Mary was spared because she hadn't overtly supported the plot in writing.

Conspirators against Elizabeth in France sent Catholic priest-in-training Gilbert Gifford to reopen communications with Mary after she was moved to a new place of imprisonment. Gifford was arrested on his arrival in England and Walsingham induced him to act as a double agent pretending to work for Mary. Gifford and other agents managed to infiltrate another plot against Elizabeth, this one led by 25-year-old lawyer-in-training Anthony Babington. Walsingham had Gifford smuggle coded messages from the group to Mary in a small waterproof wooden box hidden in beer barrels delivered to the house where she was imprisoned. Walsingham had messages from Mary brought to him to be decoded and copied by his secretary and cryptologist Thomas Phelippes, and then resealed and sent on their way. One message from Babington asked Mary to sign off on the overthrow plot, and she replied her assent.

The group was captured and, like Throckmorton, they were hung, drawn, and quartered. This time, Mary was tried and convicted, as well, although her sentence was delayed due to Elizabeth's reluctance to execute a relation and fellow queen. Mary was beheaded on February 8, 1587, a few months after the others' executions.

Walsingham also got word of an invasion plot by King Philip II of Spain. Advanced notice, in conjunction with poor weather that affected the Spanish fleet, enabled the British navy to defeat them easily.

Walsingham is considered the father of modern intelligence in England, and his espionage network is often cited as the first modern spy organization. But his spy ring didn't outlast him. He paid for many of his agents out of his own pocket without compensation from the queen. He died penniless in 1590, and his network was no more.

Q: Which ill-fated group of anti-royal revolutionaries was betrayed by a portrait?

A: The Babington Plot was an attempted coup led by Anthony Babington, in which he and several conspirators planned to assassinate Queen Elizabeth I and install Mary, Queen of Scots as queen, with help from France and Spain. Sir Francis Walsingham, Queen Elizabeth's secretary of state and spymaster, had double agents in Babington's group, but they apparently didn't know everyone involved.

Walsingham intercepted a reply from Mary giving the okay to Babington on the plan. He had his cryptologist break the code and, in that code, added a request to the letter asking for the names of all the conspirators in an attempt to get them to reveal themselves. But before Babington replied, a priest involved in the plot, Father John Ballard, was arrested. The schemers tried to run.

Unfortunately for them, their appearances were known because they had unwisely stood for a group portrait commissioned by Babington. Copies of the portrait were distributed widely to help identify and catch the conspirators. The group of would-be revolutionaries were all easily captured and put to death.

Q: Which French king set up his own covert network to secretly sway world affairs?

A: Louis XV was king of France from 1715 (when he was just 5 years old) to 1774. He set up a network of agents called the Secret du Roi (the secret of the king) in 1748, in part to push for his goals against a ministry that was heavily influenced by Cardinal Fleury.

The agents were stationed in the capitals of Europe and tasked with secretly pushing for his various political agendas, including helping his cousin, Prince Conti, to get installed as king of Poland. Conti was, in fact, the head of the Secret du Roi for a time. The king later put the Comte de Broglie in charge of his clandestine diplomacy group.

Often enough, the king's official diplomats weren't in on his secret diplomatic goals and worked at odds against the king's real motives, sowing confusion. Read on to find out about one of the Secret du Roi's most compelling agents.

Q: Which spy was ordered to live the rest of his life in France as a woman?

A: Charles-Geneviève-Louis-Auguste-André-Timothée d'Éon de Beaumont was a French aristocrat born in 1728. He excelled in many areas, including academic studies, sports, music, and fencing, and went on to study law and enter government work. D'Éon was officially hired as secretary to the French ambassador to Russia in 1756, but he was actually inducted into King Louis XV's Secret du Roi as an agent tasked with spoiling the relationship between Russia and Britain and getting Russia to help install Louis's cousin Prince Conti as king of Poland.

D'Éon disguised himself as Lia de Beaumont, niece of Chevalier Douglas, who was traveling to Russia under the cover of a geologist. D'Éon's own account of the mission varied. At one point he said Empress Elizabeth of Russia appointed Lia as her maid of honor (an unmarried woman who attends a queen or princess), and that the empress was amused when he disclosed that he was a man. However it actually went down, the ties between Russia and France strengthened, and d'Éon was offered a command in the Russian army.

The Seven Years' War between France and Britain broke out that same year and lasted until 1763. D'Éon fought as a dragoon in France's army and became a decorated war hero. He was admitted to the Order of Saint Louis for exceptional military officers, earning the title of chevalier. D'Éon and was made minister plenipotentiary (a sort of temporary ambassador). The post was cover for his reconnaissance mission to find a landing spot for an invasion and to find allies in Britain. The permanent ambassador, the Comte de Guerchy, was set to arrive months later, at which time d'Éon was to be demoted to his previous role as secretary.

The Chevalier d'Éon chafed at the idea of being Guerchy's underling and wrote angry correspondence back to France. His defiance and his extravagant spending habits got him fired, but he refused to return to France. King Louis tried to have him extradited, and the French Foreign Ministry tried to arrest him, but to no avail. D'Éon had documents on the British invasion plans, which he held over the heads of the French government. He even went so far as to publish his British diplomatic correspondence in 1764, making him a celebrity. The French government and d'Éon struck a deal that he would hand over any incriminating documents, receive an annual pension of 12,000 livres, and continue to provide France with intel on Britain.

When Louis XV died, his son Louis XVI took the throne and sent playwright Pierre Beaumarchais to convince d'Éon to return to France and hand over any other secret documents he might have. They struck yet another deal, which continued his pension and paid off his debts. But there was an unusual condition—he would be formally recognized as a woman and required to present as such.

Rumors flew all over Britain and France that d'Éon was born a woman. D'Éon may have dressed as a woman to avoid arrest. He told both an agent of the Secret du Roi and Beaumarchais that he was a woman, saying his father wanted a son and raised him as a boy. So as far as France was concerned, d'Éon had been born a woman and pretended to be a man for most of her life.

D'Éon returned to France in July 1777, at 49 years old, in his soldier's uniform (against the agreement). By royal decree, he was forced to follow the rules of the agreement months later, and Marie Antoinette's dressmaker, Rose Bertin, made d'Éon's new wardrobe! D'Éon was now officially Mademoiselle la Chevalière d'Éon.

The chevalière tried to reenlist for the American Revolutionary War but was rebuffed repeatedly and, at one point, briefly imprisoned. D'Éon returned to London in 1785. In 1789, when the French Revolution resulted in the loss of her pension, she started doing fencing exhibitions to earn money until an injury forced her to stop. She lived the rest of her life as a woman and even wrote of their moral superiority. Upon her death in 1810, it was discovered that d'Éon was born a man.

"Eonism" was used as a word for transvestism for a while, although now the term is obsolete. A British transgender support group called the Beaumont Society is also named after the Chevalière d'Éon.

CHAPTER 5

THE AMERICAS

NEW FRONTIERS AND HOMEGROWN REVOLUTIONS

Q: Which leading founding father was also a spymaster and spy?

A: As it turns out, George Washington could tell a lie—as a spy. Washington was a rich Virginia plantation heir and slaveholder who worked as a surveyor and a soldier. A volunteer mission for the royal governor of Virginia, Robert Dinwiddie, sent him to the Ohio Valley, disputed by French settlers and Virginia colonists, to deliver a command from King George II of England telling the French to leave the area. This was also an intelligence-gathering mission to find out how the French settlers were turning native tribes against colonists.

He hired experts who knew the area and could talk to the natives and the French, gained intel from Seneca Chief Half King, found the French outpost, and made a good enough impression that the French invited him to dinner, where he sipped his wine while they got drunk and spilled secrets. He and his crew even counted their canoes (some still being built) and ascertained that it might mean an attack by water. The land dispute swelled into the French and Indian War, which raged from 1754 to 1763.

At the outset of the Revolutionary War, when the patriots (who wanted to break away from British rule) fought the British and their loyalists (who wanted to remain under British rule) for independence, George Washington was made commander-in-chief of the Continental Army at the Second Continental Congress. Shortly afterward, he also became a spymaster.

A patriot group called the Sons of Liberty was already active in spy work, as were "committees of correspondence" that undertook communication between colonies, sending secret messages back and forth as fast as horses could carry their riders. But Washington made the spy work more official, setting up his own spy rings. At first, he enlisted soldiers, but after a couple of notable agents' deaths (covered in other entries in this book), he started using more civilians for intelligence gathering because they could blend in as loyalist "Tories" more easily.

Both sides of the conflict used agents and double agents, performing espionage and counterintelligence to gain information and thwart the other side's activities. Washington was disappointed to discover a mole in his midst, Dr. Benjamin Church, chief physician of the patriot army, who had acted as advisor to the Continental Congress.

Washington used subterfuge to get intelligence and protect the cover of his agents. One, a butcher and sleeper agent in New Jersey named John Honeyman, only sold his wares to "fellow" Tories to keep up his cover. Washington ordered him arrested. Honeyman resisted but was subdued and brought to the commander-in-chief. Washington gathered Honeyman's intel and staged his escape from the camp so that even Washington's own soldiers didn't know he was working for them. Washington also routinely sent off soldiers for spy work, marking them as deserters in official records for cover.

Washington knew how to use misinformation to his advantage. In one case, he went to great lengths to convince the British that the Continental Army was going to attack New York (which the British had taken early in the war) in order to divert them from attacking French troops that were about to land in Newport, Rhode Island. The French were coming to fight for the revolutionaries. Washington's play caused the British ships to return to New York as the patriots and French forces headed south to attack Virginia.

Washington also wasn't above using covert means in the pursuit of a runaway slave. When he lived in Philadelphia (at the time the capital of the new nation), he had his enslaved servants moved back to Virginia every six months to keep them from being able to claim residency in Pennsylvania and gain their freedom. Ona "Oney" Judge was one of the enslaved servants at their residence in the capital. On May 21, 1796, before Judge was to be brought back to Virginia and given as a wedding gift to Martha's reportedly ill-tempered granddaughter Elizabeth Parke Custis, Judge escaped and boarded a ship to Portsmouth, New Hampshire.

A Washington family friend (the daughter of a Senator Langdon) spotted Judge in Portsmouth, and word of her location got back to Washington, who enlisted the help of Portsmouth local Joseph Whipple. Under the ruse that he was seeking a maid, he located and spoke to Judge. Whipple tried to negotiate with Washington on her behalf. Washington refused the terms. Later, Washington asked his nephew to seize Judge (now married to a free man) and her child (who, under Virginia law, would also be enslaved). Washington's nephew told Senator Langdon, who, thankfully, warned Judge. She fled and hid with her daughter in a nearby town until the danger had passed.

Washington's enslaved workers were freed upon his death, but this didn't include Ona Judge, who was inherited from Martha's first husband and legally bound to her family. However, Judge was never caught and remained free.

Q: Which spy provided advance knowledge of England's plan to attack Philadelphia?

A: Nathaniel Sackett, head of a patriot spy ring in British-occupied New York, enlisted a woman whose identity is not known to go to New York to gather intelligence on troop movements. Her husband was a loyalist, and British troops had taken some of her grain, so she had the perfect cover: to make a complaint and ask for redress.

It's not known whom she spoke to, but she learned that the British army was constructing flat-bottomed boats to attack and occupy Philadelphia. This advance knowledge enabled members of Congress to flee to another town. It also allowed George Washington to set up a spy ring in the city before the unfortunately successful attack. The network was able to get intel to the patriots and to slip strategic bits of false information to the British army to aid the American war effort.

Q: Which famous inventor pushed propaganda and ran spy missions during the Revolutionary War?

A: Two major propaganda campaigns involved another Founding Father, Benjamin Franklin, famed scientist, inventor, printer, and politician, among his other pursuits. The British Parliament had enacted a tax on certain goods (called the Stamp Act tax because it involved stamping the items to show that the tax was paid). During protests against the tax in Boston, British soldiers fired on the crowd, killing three, including former slave Crispus Attucks. This was dubbed the Boston Massacre. The colonists' continued furor and resistance led to all but the tax on tea being dropped. Thomas Hutchinson, royal governor of Massachusetts, wrote letters to his English commanders asking for more troops and positing that it might be time to take some of the colonists' rights away. Franklin leaked the letters, and they were printed in the *Boston Gazette*, fanning the flames of revolution.

Franklin carried out his next ploy after he became the lead of the Committee for Secret Correspondence (set up by the Continental Congress for communicating with allies in other countries). He spearheaded a plan to print leaflets in German, promising free land to those who would desert the British army. These leaflets were folded to look like tobacco pouches so that they were more likely to be picked up. Patriots scattered them among the Hessians, German mercenaries working for the British military. Thousands of Hessians ended up deserting.

Benjamin Franklin didn't just leak letters and print propaganda for the war effort. He sailed to France and acted as an American diplomat, while also handling a few agents in underground missions, in his quest to convince King Louis XVI of France (husband of Marie Antoinette) to aid the Continental Army with supplies and soldiers. Franklin's spy group was infiltrated by a

British mole named Dr. Edward Bancroft, who it is speculated was known by Franklin to be a double agent and may have been used to leak information to the British.

Whether it was the diplomatic or undercover work that most swayed things in Franklin's favor, Louis XVI ended up supporting the patriots. In a bit of dark irony, the expense of helping the American revolutionaries was one of many factors that helped spark the bloody French Revolution, during which Louis XVI, Marie Antoinette, and many others lost their heads.

Q: What American speaker of famous last words was tricked into revealing his identity to British soldiers during the Revolutionary War?

A: Nathan Hale was part of an intelligence-gathering and armed-forces unit known as Knowlton's Rangers, commanded by Lieutenant Commander Thomas Knowlton and set up on George Washington's orders. Hale, a 21-year-old Yale graduate and former Connecticut school teacher turned soldier, volunteered to go behind enemy lines and spy on the British in New York. His cover was that he was a Dutch teacher, not too far from the truth.

But things went wrong. A British counterintelligence officer, Major Robert Rogers, suspected him. Dressed in civilian clothes, he approached Hale and told him he was also a spy for his side, tricking him into admitting he was a spy for the Americans. Hale was arrested and sentenced to die without trial, and at his hanging, not allowed a Bible or clergyman. He is famous for reportedly saying, "My only regret is that I have but one life to lose for my country."

Knowlton died in battle shortly before Hale's sentencing. After Knowlton and Hale's deaths, Washington changed tactics and relied more heavily on civilians than soldiers for spy work.

Q: Which people were referred to as "contraband" during the Civil War?

A: The term "contraband" for escaped slaves seeking refuge in Union camps started early in the war at Fort Monroe in Virginia, a strategic island fortress off of Hampton, Virginia, just 80 miles from Richmond, the capital of the Confederacy. General Benjamin Butler, formerly a lawyer, was in command of the fort. George Scott was one early escapee who sought refuge at the fortress, and he brought information with him. He let the Union officers know about two Confederate forts he had seen on the way, gave them a lot of detail, and led them to the locations to confirm his story. He also went out on subsequent scouting missions.

Three other escapees to the fortress were followed by a Virginia officer who demanded them back under the rules of the Fugitive Slave Act of 1850. Butler pointed out that Virginia had seceded two days earlier and said that he was "under no constitutional obligation to a foreign country." He referred to the newly arrived escapees as "contraband of war," and after that comment, former slaves who escaped to Union camps were referred to as contraband, even in official military records from the time. After this, the Union army regularly used escapees to gather intelligence for the war effort.

Incidentally, Harriet Tubman ended her wartime service at Fort Monroe.

Q: Which early Revolutionary War hero betrayed his countrymen so badly that his name is now synonymous with treachery?

A: General Benedict Arnold charged ahead of his fellow soldiers at the Second Battle of Saratoga (aka the Battle of Bemis Heights) and kept going despite being shot in the leg. He did this after being ordered not to, which may have been a red flag regarding his character. But the patriots won the battle, and Arnold was known as a hero after Saratoga.

Arnold married a 19-year-old Tory woman who was used to a lavish lifestyle. They lived beyond their means in Philadelphia, where Arnold was in charge of patriot forces. This may have contributed to the next phase of his Revolutionary War career—that of almost unbelievable treachery! From his post at Philadelphia, he got in touch with known loyalist Joseph Stansbury and offered up his services to the British as a double agent. British officer Major John André, who happened to be a friend of Arnold's wife, commanded Arnold indirectly through go-between Stansbury.

Arnold passed the British many American secrets. He then asked Washington if he could take command of West Point, a strategic fort on the Hudson River, and Washington agreed. Arnold turned right around and offered to surrender the fort to the British in exchange for 20,000 pounds, an enormous sum at the time. But Arnold's poor espionage planning got Major André captured. When Washington learned the truth about Arnold, he reportedly wept.

When he knew he was found out by his compatriots, Arnold fled to the British. Washington tried to broker a swap of André for Arnold, but the British refused, and André was hanged. Arnold became a British commander, going on to attack American forces throughout the rest of the Revolutionary War.

Despite a series of attempts by Washington to catch him, including missions led by Alexander Hamilton, Major "Light Horse Harry" Lee III, Thomas Jefferson, and the Marquis de Lafayette, Arnold was never caught. He settled in England after the war. Americans to this day refer to traitors as "Benedict Arnolds," taking some of the heat from the earlier traitor synonym Judas Iscariot.

A: Speaking of Benedict Arnold and his plot to hand West Point over to the British, his handler, Major John André of the British army, may well have been spared death if only Arnold hadn't convinced him to change into civilian clothes. For a face-to-face meeting at a safe house, André had been dropped off by a British ship (the *Vulture*) still wearing his British uniform. Arnold had concocted a cover story that the major was "John Anderson," working for Arnold as a spy, and even sent word to a nearby outpost that "Anderson" was expected and should be brought to him, just in case.

During the meeting, the *Vulture* was fired upon and retreated, leaving André without his escape route. Arnold insisted on André taking physical drawings of patriot-controlled West Point (even though André had memorized them) and convinced him to change into civilian clothes before taking off through American-held territory. André changed, stuffed the documents into his boots, and took off into the night. Arnold also gave him a handwritten pass stating that "John Anderson" was on business for Arnold and should be allowed past the guards.

After leaving the clandestine meeting, André was spotted by American militia members, whom he had unfortunately mistaken as part of his army, and he identified himself as a British soldier. When he realized his mistake, he tried to backtrack. He claimed he was Anderson and was taken to the outpost where Anderson was expected. A report was sent from there to Arnold about Anderson's arrival. Major Benjamin Tallmadge, George Washington's chief of intelligence, was suspicious of Arnold. He questioned Anderson, who claimed to be a merchant. But

Tallmadge realized the man walked like a soldier and eventually got his real identity out of him.

At the time, if you were caught in uniform, you were a prisoner of war and could not be summarily executed. But if caught as a spy, in disguise as a civilian, your true identity as a soldier was ignored, and you could be hanged. On October 2, 1780, this is exactly what happened to Major André.

Q: Which slave became a double agent during the Revolutionary War?

A: James Armistead was a slave in Virginia. He got permission from his owner, William Armistead (who was in charge of patriot military supplies in Virginia), to volunteer his services to the patriot army. James Armistead was placed in the service of the commander of the French forces, the Marquis de Lafayette, and put to work as a spy.

Armistead made his way to turncoat Benedict Arnold's British camp with a cover story that he was an escaped slave who would work for the British in exchange for his freedom. He was at first put to work as a servant, but they soon realized Armistead had knowledge of the area that could be put to use, so they appointed him to act as a spy on the patriots. So now, he was a double agent, seemingly working for the British forces of Cornwallis, but in reality working for the Americans.

He passed real intel on British forces to General Lafayette, who in turn used him to pass false information to the British. In one such case, he passed the British a document indicating that American troops were on their way to Lafayette's camp, which they were not.

Armistead was able to get word to Lafayette that Cornwallis was moving from Portsmouth to Yorktown, where he'd be joined by 10,000 British troops. This afforded Washington, Lafayette, and General Comte de Rochambeau the opportunity to set up a blockade around the Yorktown peninsula and bombard the British forces. Not long after, Cornwallis surrendered.

In 1783, Virginia passed a law offering freedom to slaves who had enlisted and contributed to the war effort. But when Armistead applied, he found that his spy work didn't qualify, so he remained enslaved. After several failed attempts at appeal, Lafayette wrote a letter in 1784 stating that Armistead's intelligence work was essential, and that he was entitled to reward. In 1787, Armistead was freed, and out of gratitude, had his name changed to James Armistead Lafayette. He also received $40 a year from Virginia for his services.

Q: What important role have clotheslines played in the historical espionage game?

A: Clotheslines make at least two significant appearances in wartime spy history. During the Revolutionary War, Anna Smith Strong, a member of the Culper Ring (one of George Washington's many spy rings), used her clothesline to send secret signals. She would hang a black petticoat if boatman Caleb Brewster was in the area, and a varying number of handkerchiefs to signal where Brewster was located. To the casual observer, it looked like she was drying laundry. But a spy looking for the signals would know what the clothing meant. The information was used to find Brewster and give him reports to be relayed, via boat and horseman, to Major Benjamin Tallmadge. Tallmadge would, in turn, hand them off to a series of couriers to relay them to Washington.

During the Civil War, a former slave named Dabney escaped to a Union camp with his wife (her name is unknown). He noticed that the Union used a flag-signaling system to send messages. He enlisted his wife to work across the Rappahannock River in enemy territory and spy on the Confederates. He and his wife came up with their own system. She would hang certain items of clothing in certain ways on a clothesline that he could see across the river. The clothes and their positions would indicate things like which way specific Confederate officers were leading their troops. He reported the information to Union officers, who made good use of the intel.

Q : Which famous escaped slave became a spy for the Union?

A : Harriet Tubman was born Araminta Ross in Maryland in the 1820s. Most people know her as an escaped slave who went on to guide other escaped slaves via a covert network called the Underground Railroad, before the Civil War ended slavery in 1865. She is sometimes referred to as Black Moses for leading people to freedom.

Under cover of night, Tubman and others in the Underground Railroad led people to safe houses called "stations". The routes were called "lines," the guides "conductors," and the coordinators for an area "station masters." The network sent coded messages calling escaped women "dry goods" and escaped men "hardware." Harriet used techniques like having escapees meet her miles away from their homes so that if they got caught shortly after they took off, she wouldn't be nearby and they wouldn't lead to her and jeopardize the whole network.

She successfully made around a dozen trips into Maryland to free people, including several family members, and she was never caught. Any escapees caught faced terrible punishment. Harriet reportedly carried a gun and threatened to shoot anyone who turned back lest they betray the rest of the group.

She also played a lead role in the rescue of Charles Nalle, a runaway caught in Troy, New York, who was about to be sent back to Virginia under the rules of the Fugitive Slave Act of 1850, which made it against federal law to help escapees, even in states that no longer allowed slavery.

All of this work was akin to spy work already. But once war broke out, Harriet became a spy for the Union in a more official capacity. Lincoln appointed William H. Seward as his secretary of state and spymaster. Seward had been an Underground Railroad station master and was a friend of Harriet's. He enlisted her, and she was given $100 in "secret service" funds to pay agents. She gathered intelligence from escaped slaves, who were fleeing in droves to Union encampments.

On June 1, 1863, she helped lead a successful raid on several South Carolina plantations with Colonel James Montgomery, making her the only woman to lead men into battle during the Civil War. They retrieved many supplies, freed and rescued slaves, and burned some of the plantations. Despite wanting to go on more attacks, she was put in charge of the rescued enslaved people brought back during the raids and never got sent back out for combat duties. General Quincy A. Gillmore, head of the Union's Department of the South, considered the intelligence she was gaining from the incoming escapees too valuable.

Unlike many African Americans who aided in the war effort, Harriet got some recognition for her contribution after the war, especially from her friend and fellow escapee Frederick Douglass. But she was never properly compensated. She had to do side work in the camps (such as laundry and baking) to earn money to help her fellow runaways. After the war, she fought to get back pay and a soldier's pension. According to official government records, she was paid only $200 for her services, plus the $100 secret service money that she had to use for agents.

Harriet Tubman is slated to appear on the new twenty-dollar bill, a spot currently held by former US President Andrew Jackson, although, as of this writing, the change has been delayed until 2026.

Q : Which Civil War spy went undercover as a birdwatcher?

A : Because the Fugitive Slave Act of 1850 made it illegal to shelter runaway slaves in the United States, Canada became an important end-point of the Underground Railroad. One of its Canadian members was Alexander Milton Ross. He was a doctor, a naturalist, an abolitionist, and a friend of Harriet Tubman.

On his own, Ross undertook the dangerous mission of going behind enemy lines into Southern states, where slavery was still legal. He would talk with plantation owners and gain permission to wander their lands, ostensibly to go birdwatching. Instead, he was seeking out the enslaved residents and giving them information on escaping to the North via the Underground Railroad.

Q: Which wealthy Southern socialite ran a spy ring to get information to the Union army?

A: Elizabeth Van Lew was a wealthy Southern woman who rightly thought slavery was cruel, freed her slaves when her father died, and rehired them as paid servants. She also ran a Union spy ring out of Richmond, Virginia.

From her property, Van Lew could see the buildings where Union soldiers were imprisoned. She volunteered as a nurse for the POWs and used the opportunity to gather information for the Union. She would give the prisoners books, where they would write intel via pinpricks before giving them back to her. She even helped some soldiers escape.

General Benjamin Butler of the Union army gave her a square cipher key, which she would use to create reports for Butler. The secret messages consisted of sequences of two-digit numbers. She kept the cipher in her watchcase, and the code was never broken by the Confederates. If spies carrying her reports were caught, the messages they carried were just numbers on a scrap of paper.

She gathered more intelligence by running a spy network consisting of a dozen or more abolitionists, Union sympathizers, and freed and still-enslaved African Americans, some working as servants in her house. They used various espionage methods to get intel and to transmit it to the Union army, like hiding messages under lion sculptures near her fireplace, to be picked up by a servant and delivered to an awaiting courier at her farm.

Van Lew further deflected suspicion by dressing oddly and mumbling and singing to herself, which made her appear unbalanced to her neighbors, garnering her the nickname Crazy Bet.

She also kept a journal, a big no-no for a spy, but she later burned it and hid or destroyed other documents because she didn't want people in her area to know of her activities that helped them lose the war. Having spent much of her money on covert wartime activities, she died penniless in 1900.

One of the slaves Van Lew freed upon her father's death was Mary Jane Richards, whose incredible exploits are revealed in the next entry.

Q: Which servant in the home of the Confederate president slipped Confederate plans to the Union army?

A: Mary Jane Richards (often erroneously called Mary "Elizabeth" Bowser) was a former slave freed by Elizabeth Van Lew. Van Lew sent her to Philadelphia for an education, and then to Liberia, a country founded as a refuge for former slaves. Richards came back to Richmond, an act that under Virginia law could have led to her re-enslavement. She married a Wilson Bowser in 1861, although the marriage didn't last.

Richards was part of Van Lew's spy network, and at some point she became a servant in the Richmond mansion that served as a home and base for Jefferson Davis, president of the Confederacy. There, Richards listened in on discussions of war plans and was able to peruse documents that were left lying out (a slave wasn't expected to be able to read).

But Richards could do even better than read them. She was reported to have had a photographic memory and could recount documents in minute detail.

As with the other stories of enslaved and formerly enslaved people spying for the Union, it is satisfying to know that the ingrained racism of the Confederate military leaders and other Southerners likely played a large part in their defeat. But unfortunately, as usual, she wasn't compensated after the war. Richards traveled north to give speeches about her work, often under pseudonyms, and taught freed slaves in Virginia and Florida, and later in St. Mary's, Georgia, where in 1867, she founded a freedman's school. That year, she married John T. Denman, and thereafter went by Mary Jane Denman.

She was inducted into the US Army intelligence Hall of Fame posthumously in 1995 as "Mary Elizabeth Bowser."

Q: Who smuggled ship plans across enemy lines in her dress during the Civil War?

A: Mary Touvestre was a free former slave in Norfolk, Virginia, working as a servant in the house of an engineer employed at the Norfolk Navy Yard. She overheard him talking about plans to resurrect the formerly sunken ship, the *Merrimack*, and to repurpose it into an ironclad warship called the *Virginia*, complete with an underwater iron ram to sink wooden Union blockade ships.

One day her employer brought home plans for the new cannon-proof beast. Touvestre hid them in her clothing, took off north, and gave them to Secretary of the Navy Gideon Welles, along with other intelligence she had gathered. The intel prompted the Union to hurry the completion and deployment of the ironclad ship the *Monitor* to stop the *Virginia* before it wreaked too much havoc on the Union Navy blockade.

Q: What enslaved ship pilot hatched a daring plan to free himself, his crew, and their families?

A: Robert Smalls was a slave whose owner hired him out to work on ships in their town of Beaufort, South Carolina (on Port Royal Island). One of these ships was a sidewheel steamship named the *Planter*, which routinely hauled supplies and ammo to Charleston, some 60 miles away by ship. On the night of May 16, 1862, after the white officers left the ship, he donned the captain's uniform and a hat as a disguise, and he and his fellow enslaved crewmembers absconded with the vessel. They stopped at a wharf to pick up his and the crew's families, and, with his knowledge of the waters and of the Confederate naval signals, he piloted the ship past multiple forts and took off for the Union blockade.

When they neared a Union ship, the *Onward*, the *Planter's* crew raised a white sheet as a flag of surrender to keep the blockade ship from firing. Captain John Frederick Nickels of the *Onward* ordered them to pull alongside. There, Smalls reportedly said to the captain, "Good morning, sir! I've brought you some of the old United States guns, sir, that were for Fort Sumter, sir."

Because he was a slave in the Antebellum South, Smalls hadn't even been officially given the title of pilot by the Confederates, although that's the job he was doing. The Union made him pilot of the ship during the war. And Robert Smalls went on to become a US congressman!

CHAPTER 6

THE GREAT WARS

WWI AND WWII

Q : What woman was instrumental in drawing the borders of the early Iraqi state?

A : British citizen Gertrude Margaret Lowthian Bell traveled the Middle East, learning the languages, gathering knowledge about the tribes and landscape, and mapping locations. She was also known to bring a fashionable wardrobe on her desert travels. On her return, she wrote a book about Syria.

Due to her extensive knowledge of the area and the people, British intelligence enlisted her to work with them in Baghdad during World War I. She would talk with (and gather information from) visiting messengers and sheiks, who were often surprised by her knowledge of their tribes.

Bell wrote a white paper explaining the area to the British government, and even drew up the borders of Iraq for them. She was for an independent Arab government, a promise made by the British during the war to gain local support. But Britain was trying to govern the area instead, going so far as to bomb towns that refused to pay taxes. This led to open rebellion.

When Churchill and others met in Cairo to finally form the postwar government, Bell was instrumental in their planning and choice of king: Faysal I, the son of Sharif Husayn of Mecca. She advised the king in the early days of his reign and went on to become Iraq's Director of Antiquities, setting up the Iraq Museum. She overdosed on sleeping pills and died on July 12, 1926. The Iraq Museum was pillaged in 2003 during the Iraq War.

Q: Which famous occultist had a hand in sinking the passenger ship *Lusitania* in 1915?

A: Aleister Crowley is best known for his foray into the occult, but he also claimed to work as a spy for the British during World War I. He was reportedly tasked with helping get the United States involved in the war, and to this aim, he insinuated himself into the German spy network as a double agent. Crowley traveled to America in the guise of an anti-British Irish revolutionary and tore up a fake British passport in an outward show of protest. Germany was all for Irish revolt, and this gave Crowley an in.

He got a job writing for the magazine *The Fatherland*, part of the German Propaganda Kabinett, a group whose aim was to keep the US neutral in the war. Crowley attended a March 1915 Kabinett meeting, convincing the Germans that he had insight into the psychology of the Americans, and that they admired arrogance and violence. The *Lusitania* was a passenger liner that was also being used to ship war supplies from New York to England. When they asked Crowley if sinking the ship would tip America against them, he said no, and this opinion was sent to Berlin.

On May 7, 1915, around 12 miles off the coast of Ireland, a German U-20 submarine (U-boat) fired a torpedo at the *Lusitania*, sinking it and killing 1,198 people. It was an infamous act that did, indeed, turn Americans against Germany, although the act didn't get the US into the war right away (the tipping point was the telegram in the next entry). Crowley went on to spy for Britain during World War II, as well.

Q: What intercepted telegram convinced the US to join World War I?

A: German Foreign Minister Arthur Zimmermann sent a message dubbed the "Zimmermann telegram" on January 16, 1917 to German Minister to Mexico Heinrich von Eckhardt (via German Ambassador to the US Count von Bernstorff in Washington, DC). The telegram instructed the ambassador to try to enlist the help of Mexico during the war in exchange for the parts of the United States it had lost (Texas, New Mexico, and Arizona) and also suggested getting Japan involved.

British intelligence intercepted the message and cryptographers in Room 40 of the Old London Admiralty Building (run by Reginald Blinker Hall) decoded it. To hide the fact that Britain had broken this particular code, British intelligence located the telegram received on the Mexican side so that they could pretend they had only broken that less complicated code.

President Woodrow Wilson learned of the information and had it published in the papers. Knowledge of the plot turned American public opinion solidly against the Germans. On April 6, 1917, President Wilson declared war on Germany.

Q: Which famous dancer is remembered for her short, ill-fated career as a double agent?

A: Mata Hari, born in 1895 in the Netherlands as Margaretha Geertruida Zelle, is likely the most famous female spy in history. But her real career in espionage was short and tragic. She married Rudolf MacLeod, a soldier posted in the Dutch East Indies (now Indonesia), after answering an ad he had placed looking for a wife. After a failed marriage, he got custody of their daughter and Mata Hari settled in Paris. She became a self-styled exotic dancer and courtesan who embarked on a series of affairs, some with high-ranking officials on both sides of WWI. Because of this, France and Britain put her under surveillance.

She was inducted into the spy world when, during WWI, she requested permission from France to travel to a restricted war zone in Vittel, France, to visit her wounded Russian lover in the hospital. France offered her 1 million francs to spy for them by seducing a high-ranking German commander, but she was detained in England on the way.

She then traveled to Madrid, Spain, and became romantically involved with a German military attaché, Arnold Kalle, to whom she reportedly only gave gossip and newspaper articles rather than real information. Kalle sent a message to Germany, in a code he knew the French had deciphered, saying H-21 (her designation) had been useful, possibly with the aim of getting her arrested. This led to her arrest in Paris for spying for the Germans. She did admit to taking some money from Germany, but said that she never divulged any real secrets to them and that she considered it compensation for property they had seized from her earlier.

In February 1917, Mata Hari was convicted of eight counts of espionage, likely with the help of forged evidence, including charges that she gave the Germans information about a new Allied tank and caused the deaths of tens of thousands of soldiers. She was executed on October 15, 1917. She refused a blindfold and, according to legend, blew a kiss to the firing squad. Germany officially cleared her name in 1930.

Q: Which languages were used by the US during WWII to send coded messages that were never broken by Axis powers?

A: The US enlisted people of the Navajo Native American tribe to help send coded communications starting in WWI, but especially during WWII. Navajo is a tonal language (different tones can change the meaning of a word) with no alphabet. Fewer than thirty Americans who weren't Navajo knew the language in the 1940s. One of them, Philip Johnston, who grew up in a missionary family on a reservation, suggested hiring Navajos as radio operators during the war. Eventually, more than four hundred Navajo soldiers worked with the US Marines in the Pacific, and they were referred to as code talkers. For words that didn't exist in Navajo, they had to get creative, with substitutions like their word for "our mother" for the US and the word for "tortoise" for tank.

Navajo wasn't the only Native American language used in WWII. In Europe, the code talkers were of the Comanche tribe. The Comanche had to similarly improvise for words that didn't exist in their language, with words such as "jump soldiers" for parachuters and the funny and appropriate "crazy white man" for Hitler.

Germany and Japan found the languages impossible to crack. During the Battle of Iwo Jima, six Navajo sent over eight hundred messages in the first two days.

The code talkers didn't receive recognition for their contribution until the program was declassified in 1968.

Q: Which famous American actress was also a spy for the French Resistance?

A: Josephine Baker (née Freda Josephine McDonald) was a dancer, singer, and actress from Missouri who emigrated from the US to France in 1925. In Paris, she became a huge dance-hall star and didn't encounter the level of racism that she had in the US.

At the start of WWII, she fled Paris for the South of France. She worked with the Red Cross and was recruited into the French Resistance by Jacques Abtey, head of French counter-military intelligence. Baker took in resistance fighters and attended parties where she could hobnob with Axis diplomats and gather intelligence.

Her celebrity largely protected her, but after Nazis showed up to question her at her home, she fled to England, with intel written on her sheet music in invisible ink.

After the war, she was awarded the Croix de Guerre and named Chevalier de Légion d'honneur with the Rosette de la Résistance by General Charles de Gaulle.

She returned to the US periodically to protest during the Civil Rights Movement. Josephine Baker died in France in 1975.

Q: Which famous fashion designer worked for a unit whose sole job was to trick the Axis armies during World War II?

A: Bill Blass was one of 1,100 or so members of the 23rd Headquarters Special Troops, colloquially referred to as the Ghost Army, during WWII. The unit used a mix of real and fake equipment (including inflatable tanks and planes), advanced audio equipment blaring expertly recorded sounds, and fake versions of real units' vehicle insignias and uniform patches to trick the enemy into thinking an active combat unit was in an area while the real unit was on its way elsewhere.

Many of the members were artists and actors. The actors would do things like imitate real units' radio operators, dress up as and imitate real generals, and go into cafés and speak misinformation for any spies who might be nearby.

The very existence of the Ghost Army was classified until 1996. It is estimated that they contributed to several victories and saved thousands of Allied soldiers' lives.

Q: How did the intelligence term "Fifth Column" originate?

A: The term "Fifth Column" refers to a group of conspirators within a country who are actually working for the country's enemy. But its original use was propaganda, not a real conspiracy.

The phrase came from one of Franco's generals during the Spanish Civil War in 1936. When he was about to attack Madrid, he announced that four columns of his soldiers were advancing on Madrid, and a fifth column already lay in wait inside the city. His aim was to scare Madrid's soldiers. But this fifth column didn't actually exist.

Q: Which false flag operation kicked off WWII in Asia?

A: The Mukden Incident (also referred to as the Manchurian Incident) involved an explosion in Kwantung (Guandong), China, on September 18, 1931. Someone used explosives to blow a small gap in the South Manchurian Railway near a Japanese base. The Japanese decried the seemingly terrorist attack as an act of aggression by China and used it as an excuse to occupy the province where it happened and rename it Manchukuo.

But the Japanese military set off the explosion themselves, apparently without the approval of the government of Japan, and then began to expand their military presence throughout Manchuria, outside the purview of Prime Minister Wakatsuki Reijiro and the Japanese army leaders.

At the time of the event, China asked the League of Nations to intervene, and the Lytton Commission investigated and criticized Japan's actions. Japan simply left the League and continued with their hostilities against China.

After the war, testimony in a war crimes trial in Tokyo from 1946 to 1948 revealed the ruse. The incident sparked WWII on the Pacific stage.

A : On August 31, 1939, one of Germany's radio stations in Gleiwitz near the German and Polish border was apparently attacked and taken over. The "aggressors" then gave a short anti-German speech over the radio in Polish.

But the attackers weren't Polish. In fact, there was no attack. Germans, led by SS officer Alfred Helmut Naujocks, had kidnapped and drugged a Polish farmer (referred to in the Nazi plan as "canned meat"), put him in a Polish military uniform, taken him to the German radio station, and shot him to make it look like Poland had initiated hostilities with Germany. They also left bodies of several convicts at the station.

They used this as a pretext to invade Poland, kicking off WWII on the European stage.

Q: Where did the saying "loose lips sink ships" originate?

A: During WWII, the US War Department had the Office of War Information (OWI) make a series of propaganda posters that volunteers pasted up all over the US. A poster that read "Loose Lips Might Sink Ships" and had a picture of a smoking, sinking vessel was one of many warnings to citizens about the dangers of making remarks or writing about soldiers shipping out, troop destinations, war equipment, or anything similar that could be overheard or intercepted by spies of the enemy.

Q: Which Japanese agent gained intelligence from a US airbase?

A: Naval intelligence officer Takeo Yoshikawa was sent undercover to the Japanese consulate in Honolulu, Hawaii. He pretended to be an unserious employee just out for a good time, but he was really scouting the island and gathering intelligence for Japan on details of the US's naval force. On one occasion, he even visited Wheeler Air Force Base with a group of tourists— they were having an open house! He also took a tourist flight to survey the island.

He wasn't the only Japanese consulate staffer to use apparent tourist activity to gather intelligence on the US military. Another consulate staffer in Honolulu traveled around in a taxi with a copy of *Jane's Fighting Ships* (an annual catalog of naval ships from around the world) and toured the area surrounding the base at Pearl Harbor.

Q: Geniuses working at Bletchley Park cracked what German machine's coded messages?

A: German engineer Arthur Scherbius developed the Enigma machine in the 1920s. It electronically and mechanically encrypted any message entered, and its settings changed for the next message. At first, only someone with another Enigma machine and knowledge of the settings for the original message could decode them. Germany considered it impossible to crack.

In 1932, France gave Poland operator's manuals and a list of settings for the previous few months for an Enigma machine that they had gotten from a German code clerk. Poland was able to use the information to make a replica Enigma machine. By 1938, they were able to decrypt as much as 75 percent of Germany's Enigma-produced messages, until Germany improved the Enigma machine.

Poland gave their work, including copies of the machines, to France and Britain. The British government set up Operation Ultra in their communication headquarters, a mansion called Bletchley Park. A large group of linguists, mathematicians, chess players, and other puzzle solvers worked there, possibly up to ten thousand in all, including a larger group of women than were allowed in most wartime departments. Many had been recruited by people who had them solve puzzles to test them on the sly.

For around five years, the group used a large device they called the Bombe to replicate the workings of an Enigma machine and decode Enigma messages. Germany never figured out that their Enigma machine had been cracked. The workers at Bletchley Park were sworn to absolute secrecy and managed to keep it secret until the operation was declassified in the 1970s.

The team at Bletchley Park deciphered so much good intel that the Allies had to ignore some impending attacks so that the Germans wouldn't catch on that they had deciphered Enigma. It is speculated that the intel gathered at Bletchley Park may have shortened the duration of the war by as much as two years and saved countless lives.

Alan Turing, Cambridge mathematician famous for breakthroughs in computing (including the idea of using binary code), was the lead codebreaker at Bletchley Park. Sadly, he was persecuted by the very government he worked to defend under antiquarian anti-homosexuality laws. Turing was forced to "chemically castrate" himself by taking estrogen. He died at the age of 41 on June 7, 1954, of cyanide poisoning. His death was ruled a suicide.

Q: Which spy was the most highly decorated female civilian in WWII?

A: Virginia "Dindy" Hall, born 1906 to a wealthy family in Baltimore, Maryland, was considered by the Gestapo to be one of the Allies' most dangerous spies. She studied languages, becoming fluent in German, Italian, and French, and at 25 got a job as a clerk at the American embassy in Poland. While hunting birds with friends, she accidentally shot herself in the foot, and her leg had to be amputated due to gangrene. She got a wooden leg and nicknamed it Cuthbert. This gave her a limp that the Germans later identified.

She was in Paris when WWI erupted. She volunteered as an ambulance driver, but fled to London when Germany overtook France. There, she joined the Special Operations Executive (SOE), trained briefly, and was sent back to France under the cover of a journalist for the *New York Post*. She worked from a convent in Lyon, where she enlisted the help of the nuns. She also gathered intel from the workers at a brothel.

Hall organized the resistance in Vichy, France, arranging safe houses and dead drops. She also helped flyers downed behind enemy lines and escaped POWs flee to safety. She changed her appearance frequently, but the Gestapo realized at some point that they were looking for a woman with a limp. Klaus Barbie, the Butcher of Lyon, was pursuing her.

In winter of 1941, Hall and three others fled over the mountains to Spain, where she was arrested and held for six weeks. Upon release, she returned to England. The SOE didn't want to send her back to France because of the danger, so she joined the American Office of Strategic Services (OSS) in 1943.

Hall dyed her hair, had her teeth ground down, learned from a makeup artist how to make herself look older, packed bulky, unflattering clothes, and went back to France, where she operated from 1944 to 1945. There, she trained units of agents (totaling in the hundreds) and took them on a sabotage spree, blowing up bridges and rail lines and disrupting communications. She spied on the Germans as a goat-herding peasant and radioed information back to England.

She was never caught, and after the war became the only civilian woman to receive the Distinguished Service Cross from the OSS. She joined the CIA and worked there for fifteen years. She kept her service during the war quiet and died in 1982.

Q: Which SOE operative became the only radio operator in France after the others were captured?

A: Inayat Khan was a Muslim from India and a descendant of Indian ruler Tipu Sultan, who taught Sufism and Sufi music. He went to the United States to spread the Sufi message and met Ora Ray Baker. Khan proposed. Ora's brother Perry Baker, a yoga teacher and Ora's guardian, did not approve. Khan left for England and Ora followed shortly thereafter. The couple wed there. He taught throughout Europe, and in 1914, the couple's daughter, Noor Inayat Khan (or Noor-un-Nissa, "light among women"), was born in St. Petersburg, Russia.

A patron of Inayat Khan gave his family a house in Suresnes, France, and they settled there when Noor was 8 years old. Between the wars, many were attracted to her father's Sufi teachings, which included the idea of a path to service in the world. Her father died in India when she was 13. Thereafter, she took care of her siblings and her mother. She also published a book of children's stories titled *Twenty Jataka Tales*.

When the Nazis occupied France, the family fled to England. There, Noor Khan joined the British Women's Auxiliary Air Force and worked as a radio operator, sending and receiving messages in Morse code. When she tried to transfer to Winston Churchill's Special Operations Executive (SOE), her superiors gave her a negative review, citing idealism, refusal to lie, and lack of focus when translating coded messages, among other things, which got her rejected initially.

But Maurice Buckmaster, head of the F (France) Section of the SOE, needed radio operators, especially those fluent in French. He saw the poor review and intervened. Buckmaster tasked Leo Marks, the SOE's 22-year-old head of communications and chief cryptologist, with training her in codes and reevaluating her performance. Noor's coding skills improved under his tutelage, and she was accepted into the F Section.

She and Marks agreed on a "bluff check" so that the SOE could tell from her messages if she'd been captured. And any German agent pretending to be her wouldn't know the bluff.

On June 16, 1943, she was flown into Paris at night. Her alias was Jeanne Marie Renier (code name Madeleine), and her cover story was that she was a children's nurse. But she would really be a radio operator for the Prosper Network, the largest SOE group in France, headquartered in the National School of Agriculture near Versailles. It handled communications between the French Resistance and London. The leader of the network was Francis Suttill, code-named Prosper.

Noor settled in more quickly than most agents and sent her first communication back to London in seventy-two hours.

Wireless operator was considered one of the most dangerous jobs in wartime intelligence. The Nazis had direction-finding equipment in vans that could pinpoint an agent's location within fifteen to twenty minutes, so they had to work in short increments. There was apparently a saying that the life of a wireless operator was six minutes.

Noor lasted considerably longer than that, but her career nearly came to an end a mere six days into her mission. A man in the resistance who had met her plane, Henri Déricourt, is thought to have been a double agent for the SOE and the Abwehr (German counterintelligence). The Gestapo started arresting or killing Prosper agents six days after Noor arrived. They got all the other radio operators plus Suttill, who was taken to Gestapo headquarters in Paris and interrogated until he gave up information on hidden weapons and explosives. Suttill was imprisoned in the

Sachsenhausen concentration camp for two years and executed in 1945.

Noor got a warning before the rest were captured and rode her bike to Paris, where resistance agents got her into a safe house. She was not just the only one left from the Prosper group, she was the only SOE radio operator left in Paris! She set up the radio and antenna (a long wire that had to be strung up before each communication) and radioed back to London that Prosper had fallen. Buckmaster offered to get her back to Britain for her safety, but she refused.

Noor continued to coordinate weapons drops and escapes of Allied airmen who had been downed. She had to carry the radio equipment from place to place with her, and, when she knew the Gestapo had learned what she looked like, to change her appearance to avoid capture. Once, an officer caught her setting up her antenna outdoors, and she convinced him she was setting it up to play music.

At some point, the Gestapo started offering money for people to denounce others. After Noor had been there four months, a woman named Renée Garry, sister of Émile Garry, the man who ran the network Noor now worked for, betrayed her and gave them the location of her apartment. She and her codebook were captured on October 13, 1943.

At Gestapo headquarters, she went through three weeks of interrogation. She refused to give anyone up, but they had her codebook and used it to send messages back to the SOE in London. It was a while before Marks and Buckmaster were notified of a disparity in the bluff check.

Noor planned an escape with two other prisoners via secret notes they left in the bathroom they shared, and a screwdriver one stole and hid in the bathroom. They each used it to loosen the bars on their windows. All three managed to escape to the roof. But a Royal Air Force air raid prompted the guards to check on the prisoners, and the escapees were captured.

Lead interrogator Hans Kieffer had Noor classified as Nacht und Nebel ("night and fog"), which meant she was dangerous and should be made to disappear. On November 6, 1943, Noor was sent to Pforzheim prison in Germany. A year later she was transferred to Dachau, where she was executed.

Noor was posthumously awarded the Croix de Guerre by the French and the George Cross by the British. A memorial bust of Noor Inayat Khan was installed at Gordon Square in London in 2012. A plaque at Dachau also commemorates her.

Q: Which member of the SOE had a million-franc bounty on her head?

A: Cecile Pearl Witherington was another member of Churchill's SOE. She smuggled weapons into France to help with the resistance against Nazi occupiers. During one mission, her superior officer was arrested, and Witherington took charge and led the others into a fourteen-hour attack.

Germany put a bounty on her head of 1 million francs, but fortunately, no one claimed it. She lived to the ripe old age of 93.

Q: Which future chef worked on developing shark repellent for the OSS during WWII?

A: Julia McWilliams joined the OSS after Pearl Harbor was bombed. She later described her role as that of a file clerk, but she dealt with personnel and was even at one point enlisted to help create shark repellant. She was sent from Washington DC to work in India, and then China. McWilliams married fellow OSS agent Paul Child.

Now her name was Julia Child, and after the war, she became a cookbook author and distinctive television persona famous for instructing the world how to cook French cuisine.

Q: Who ran a group of fake agents that misled Germany into thinking forces were landing at Pas-de-Calais, France, on D-Day?

A: Juan Pujol Garcia (code name "Garbo") was a Spanish citizen who attempted to offer his services as an agent to British intelligence in Madrid and Lisbon several times starting in 1941. They wouldn't talk to him, so he went and joined the German Abwehr military intelligence via their agents in Madrid. He told them he had business in London, and they ordered him to set up a spy ring there.

Instead, he returned to Lisbon, continued trying to get in touch with British intelligence, made up a few fake agents, created reports using reference books about England, and sent them to the Germans. In April 1942, MI6 finally took notice and sent him to London.

He was put under the charge of a handler named Tomás Harris. Together, they created twenty-seven fake agents who would send false information to German intelligence in an effort to mislead them on Allied plans.

One of his big successes involved a major moment in the war. Germany guessed that Allied forces were either going to be landing at Normandy or Pas-de-Calais, both on the northern coast of France. Britain made up something called the First US Army Group, and Garbo put out misinformation that this fictional group was stationed in East Anglia, which would have made a landing at Pas-de-Calais most likely.

Allied forces didn't just stop with misinformation. They stationed the 23rd Headquarters Special Troops in East Anglia. This group, called the Ghost Army, deceived Axis intelligence with fake buildings, inflatable tanks, and actors pretending to be soldiers. They broadcast fake radio transmissions and played audio recordings to make it sound like an active unit, often adding the insignias of other units to their vehicles and clothing. If a German plane flew over, the dummy unit would look and sound like a real active military presence.

On June 6, 1944, the Allies stormed the beach at Normandy, an event known as D-Day. Most of the German forces (maybe as many as 300,000 troops) were waiting at Pas-de-Calais.

Q: What famous but ill-fated pilot is thought to have been one of the spies investigating Japan's military buildup in the Pacific?

A: Germany's territories were doled out to the victors after they lost WWI under the Treaty of Versailles. Several Pacific Islands (the Carolines, Marshall Islands, and the Mariana islands) went to Japan. In the early days of WWII, Japan started building up their military presence on the islands, including building airfields.

The US sent agents to investigate. One is thought to have been Amelia Earhart. She is most famous for traversing the Atlantic in 1932, but going missing in 1937. Her flight path came close to these Japanese-controlled islands. It is not known for sure that she was spying. It could have been a coincidence. But some US agents did indeed disappear on their mission to surveil these islands.

Q: What Swedish official helped as many as 100,000 Jewish people escape the Nazis?

A: Raoul Wallenberg was a Swedish official stationed in Hungary. He provided Swedish passports to a great many Jewish people and sheltered them in buildings designated as property of Sweden. He is credited with saving as many as 100,000 Hungarian Jews.

Unfortunately, Wallenberg met a tragic end. He was captured by Russian forces when they invaded Hungary. Stalin, being the paranoid sort, had Wallenberg tortured and poisoned due to his amazing skills at deception.

Q: What fictional agent was used to fool the Germans into thinking the Allies were landing in Greece?

A: During WWII, around April 30, 1943, a Spanish fisherman found the corpse of a British soldier. Around that same time, a news release from Britain stated that a plane transporting British officers had gone down in the area. The body had dog tags and other documents indicating that he was Major William Martin of the Royal Marines. He was in a British uniform, wearing a life jacket, and had a briefcase handcuffed to his wrist. Spain informed the British authorities but first allowed Nazi spies to photograph the documents in the briefcase (they even unsealed and resealed envelopes). The documents detailed an Allied plan called Operation Husky to land forces in Greece rather than Italy as originally planned.

But Major Martin wasn't a real soldier. He was a homeless man named Glyndwr Michael, who had died after ingesting rat poison. British intelligence officers Charles Cholmondeley and Ewen Montagu dressed him up and had him tossed off a surfaced submarine near the coast of Spain. The Allies really intended to land in Sicily but wanted to throw off the Germans so that they couldn't mount a large defense. They dubbed the plan Operation Mincemeat, and when messages decrypted at Bletchley Park indicated that German command in Berlin believed the false information, they sent a telegram to Churchill that read, "Mincemeat swallowed hook, line, and sinker." The bulk of the German forces were diverted to Greece, and the allies met little resistance when they landed at Sicily.

Incidentally, Ian Fleming, future author of the James Bond series, came up with the idea for Operation Mincemeat when he was with British intelligence.

CHAPTER 7

NEW WARS, COLD AND HOT

THE ANTI-COMMUNIST CONFLICTS

Q: Which engineer, famous for music, invented an advanced listening device that remained undetected in an ambassador's office for years?

A: In 1919, Russian scientist, engineer, and amateur cellist Léon Theremin invented an electronic musical instrument that still bears his name—the Theremin. A musician plays it by moving their hands near two antennae, causing it to emit ethereal electronic sounds. He was invited to demonstrate the device to none other than Bolshevik leader Vladimir Ilyich Lenin. He was then sent on a tour of Russia, Europe, and the United States to show off his invention (and also to gather intelligence, according to biographer Albert Glinsky, who called the music tour a Trojan horse).

RCA licensed the right to manufacture the Theremin and put it on sale in 1929, just before the stock market crash. The instrument and Theramin's various other inventions didn't take off, and he got into financial difficulties. His marriage to ballet dancer Lavinia Williams in 1938 exacerbated his problems due to loss of sponsorships (she was African American, and racism abounded in the US).

One day, he disappeared. His wife and friends didn't know what happened to him. Some people assumed he was captured by the Soviets and taken back to Russia, but according to Glinsky, he had voluntarily returned to his home country. In either case, unfortunately for Theremin, Stalin had him imprisoned in the Gulag in Siberia, then taken, still as prisoner, to Moscow to work on inventions for the Soviet Union. These inventions included listening devices, or "bugs."

One of these bugs was later dubbed "The Thing" by US intelligence. Schoolchildren presented a 2-foot-diameter carved wooden seal of the United States to US ambassador to Russia,

Averill Harriman, in 1946. He hung the gift in his office, not knowing that it held a secret.

In 1952, a listening device like no other Western intelligence had ever seen was found inside the seal. It was remarkably advanced and didn't require a direct power source, but was instead triggered by beams that turned it into an active microphone. Nearby Russian agents had been listening in on conversations in the ambassador's office for six years! British and American intelligence copied the device and used it against the Soviets.

Theremin was released from imprisonment in 1947 and continued to work in Russia.

Theremin's instrument was later used in 1950s sci-fi movie soundtracks like *The Day the Earth Stood Still*, and a related instrument was used by the Beach Boys on their hit song "Good Vibrations."

Q: What were the Venona Decrypts?

A: The Venona Decrypts were messages decoded as part of the Venona Project, a wartime project that the Army Signal Intelligence Services (SIS) and FBI started in August 1943. It continued into the Cold War and, eventually, the National Security Agency (NSA) took over it. The project consisted of an effort to decrypt telegrams sent from the Soviet embassy and consulates in the US. Even after WWII, Venona Project cryptographers kept trying to crack the massive backlog of wartime messages that had been collected.

In 1946, the Russians made a mistake and reused individual pages of one-time-use pads, which involved sets of random numbers and a one-time-use key exchanged by the sender and receiver of the message to encode and translate it. The reused pads enabled cryptographers to decipher some patterns and interpret messages. Some of the Bletchley Park decoders worked on the project.

The Venona Decrypts incriminated Donald Maclean of the Cambridge Five (see page 125) and Klaus Fuchs, a German researcher at Los Alamos. Both were working for the Soviets. Some telegrams decoded in 1996 also provided further evidence against Alger Hiss, a State Department official who had advised Franklin Delano Roosevelt on the building of the United Nations after WWII and accompanied him to talks at Yalta. Hiss was also a Soviet agent.

Like Bletchley Park, the Venona Project was a closely held secret, so secret that even President Truman didn't know the details of the operation. But he was informed about the information they decoded.

Q: Which agent convinced the CIA to supply him with a suicide pill?

A: Aleksandr Dmitrievich Ogorodnik, code-named TRIGON, was a Soviet diplomat in Bogotá, Colombia, in the mid-1980s. He volunteered to spy for the CIA due to the damage done to his family during the Stalinist purges of the 1930s, and continued to pass intel after he was transferred back to Moscow.

A few years later, he asked his handler, Jack Downing, the CIA chief in Moscow, for a suicide pill. If the KGB caught him, he wanted to end it quickly rather than be subjected to torture. Downing refused at first, because that was way outside normal CIA protocol. But Ogorodnik refused to provide any more intelligence without a suicide pill, so the US relented and gave him a ballpoint pen with a suicide capsule embedded on one end. The KGB eventually caught him, and he immediately bit off the capsule and died.

Q: Which Soviet intelligence officer offered to spy for the US in part because he needed money for his girlfriend's abortion?

A: Pyotr Popov was a major in the GRU (the Soviet Union's military intelligence branch). He was also a peasant who had bitter feelings about earlier Russian and then Soviet intelligence agencies that had done nothing positive for the people in the area from which he came. He was also in need of money to get his pregnant Serbian girlfriend an abortion (he also had a wife).

While in Vienna, Austria, in 1952, Popov deposited a letter offering his services in a US diplomat's car. He spied for the US from posts in both Vienna and Berlin, from 1953 to 1958, handled by CIA agent George Kisevalter, who had to wrangle Popov due to his reckless behavior and disregard for safety measures.

Unfortunately for Popov, once in Berlin, he is thought to have been betrayed by a Russian mole in the British Military Intelligence Section 6 (MI6), George Blake.

Q: What secret tunnel in Berlin turned out not to be much of a secret?

A: In 1955, the CIA and MI6 built a nearly 600-yard underground tunnel from the American zone into the Soviet zone of West Berlin, an effort dubbed "Operation Gold." The head of the CIA's Berlin Operations Base (BOB), William King Harvey, conceived the idea as an alternative to recruiting Soviet spies. The tunnel itself came to be known as the Berlin Tunnel.

BOB operatives built a warehouse on the American side to conceal the work and contain the dirt they were displacing. They sprayed chemicals on the machinery to keep it from making too much noise. And they air-conditioned the tunnel to counter the heat thrown off by electronic lines so that the winter snow above wouldn't melt and reveal that something was odd about the area.

Once the tunnel was complete, they had MI6 tap the telephone lines. British and American intelligence listened in on and recorded communications from East Berlin to Russia and elsewhere over around 430 phone lines.

But the tunnel wasn't as much of a secret as the CIA and MI6 thought. The Soviets knew they were working on it due to information from George Blake, a Soviet mole in the MI6. Soviet officials under Nikita Khrushchev let it run for over thirteen months and then pretended to discover it in 1956. Remarkably, from information divulged by officials under Boris Yeltsin's government, it is thought that Khrushchev's government made no effort to alter communications from Berlin, possibly because of the difficulty involved and possibly so as not to draw attention to Blake.

Q: Which US governmental body had its own secret nuclear bunker during the Cold War?

A: Between 1958 and 1961, a 112,544-square-foot underground bunker was built in the West Virginia mountains underneath the Greenbrier Resort Hotel. This extremely secret project, code-named "Project Greek Island," was meant to shelter the US Congress in the event of a nuclear war. Employees working undercover as Forsythe Associates staff, a dummy company providing audiovisual support to the hotel, kept the bunker at the ready. Construction of a hotel wing was used as cover for construction of the bunker, which was built underneath the new wing. The site remained active for thirty years. The *Washington Post* exposed the secret on May 31, 1992.

The bunker had a 25-ton blast door, decontamination chambers, living space for 1,100 people, a cafeteria, an infirmary with twelve hospital beds, an ICU, a laboratory, a pharmacy, meeting spaces, and TV and recording studios with backdrops of real locations in US cities so officials could broadcast out to citizens living aboveground without revealing their location. It was also equipped with its own power plant, diesel storage tanks, and water-purification equipment. The site has since been decommissioned and is now open to the public for tours.

Q: Which ring of moles for the Soviet Union rose to great heights in British intelligence?

A: The Cambridge Five, a group of four Cambridge students and one tutor, were recruited to the Soviet cause in the 1930s by Arnold Deutsch, a professor at Cambridge who also happened to be a spy for the Soviets. The group consisted of Kim Philby, Guy Burgess, Donald Maclean, Anthony Blunt, and John Cairncross.

They were all disillusioned by the post-Depression toll on the everyday British citizen compared to the wealth they were seeing at Cambridge, and Deutsch presented the Soviet system as an alternative to rampant capitalism. Philby also later said he thought that the USSR was the only power strong enough to counter the fascism sweeping Europe.

All became employed in British intelligence, Blunt in MI5, Philby in MI6, Burgess in MI6 and the SOE, Maclean in the Foreign Office, and Cairncross in the office of the minister of intelligence services. The group passed secrets to the Soviets on Operation Rollback (the effort to contain and roll back Stalinist communism), nuclear weapons, and agents working for the West.

Maclean became first secretary at the British embassy in Washington, DC, in 1944, and in 1950, Burgess became second secretary at the embassy. Philby rose to head of Soviet counterintelligence at MI6 and in 1949 was stationed in Washington, as liaison between MI6 and the FBI and CIA, where he was updated on high-level American as well as British secrets. He also befriended the head of the CIA Office of Strategic Operations, James Jesus Angleton.

Philby knew about the Venona Decrypts (part of a long-term effort to decrypt coded messages out of the Russian embassy) and was able to warn Donald Maclean that he was found out, leading

Maclean and Burgess to flee to Russia in 1951. Cairncross also resigned.

After the revelations about his compatriots, Philby came under suspicion and resigned from MI6, but he was exonerated by an internal investigation and continued to do some work for MI6. In 1963, when new suspicions of his duplicity arose, he fled to the Soviet Union. Blunt was then confronted in 1964, and he admitted his KGB service and gave secrets about their operations. He was stripped of the knighthood awarded to him earlier in his service. None of the group was ever prosecuted.

Philby wrote a memoir titled *My Silent War* about his time as a spy. The Soviets gave him the rank of KGB General, awarded him the Order of the Red Banner, and put him on a postage stamp. He lived out the rest of his days in Russia and died in 1988.

A: In 1962, Nikita Khrushchev made an attempt to set up nuclear bases in Cuba, nerve-rackingly close to the United States. The US found out when the CIA's U-2 spy planes photographed the bases' construction. Tensions ran so high between the US and the Soviets that some think it was the closest we've ever come to nuclear conflict. But Premier Khrushchev and President Kennedy talked, tensions eased, and the crisis was averted. The event has since been dubbed the Cuban Missile Crisis.

Kennedy's worries were lessened when Oleg Penkovsky, a high official in the Soviet military, who also happened to be a volunteer spy for the US and Britain, revealed that the US was ahead of the Soviets in missile capability, that Khrushchev was isolated politically in Russia, and that he was probably posturing. President Kennedy got a similar assessment from Llewellyn Thompson, a former ambassador to the USSR. The reports gave the president confidence in the idea that he could set up a naval blockade rather than invade Cuba, which gave him and Khrushchev a chance to talk it out.

Tensions between Russia and the US lessened even further in the late 1960s during a period of détente, although spying and one-upmanship continued.

Q: Which high Russian military official volunteered to spy for the United States and Britain?

A: Colonel Oleg Penkovsky was an officer of the GRU (the Soviet Union's military intelligence branch). His father had been an anti-Bolshevik fighter for the Russian White Army during the Russian Civil War. He also came from money. He believed both of these facts hurt his chances of success in Bolshevik Russia.

At his post in Turkey, Penkovsky had befriended Colonel Charles MacLean Peeke, an attaché with the US Army, which contributed to his favorable view of the West. He decided to ally himself with a Western intelligence agency.

He had access to high-level military intelligence, but he couldn't get a meeting with any US official. In August 1960, he found two American tourists on the Moskvoretsky Bridge and asked them to get a bundle of military intelligence to a US embassy official for him. While he was waiting, he also tried to contact British and Canadian officials, to no avail.

But the US eventually took him up on his offer, and he worked for both MI6 and the CIA under the code name Hero. He photographed secret documents with a Minox camera and slipped intel to a British diplomat's wife, Janet Chisholm, via brush passes in Moscow (some of which it turned out were photographed by KGB agents), and left information at a dead drop behind a radiator in an apartment building (using both methods far longer than was advisable).

He was handled by CIA agents George Kisevalter and Joseph Bulik, and MI6 agents Michael Stokes and Harold Shergold, who tried to persuade him to be more cautious. Greville Wynne, a British businessman, acted as a courier to and from Penkovsky.

Penkovsky gave MI6 and the CIA over ten thousand pages of Soviet military intel. He also provided information on Khrushchev's actual military capabilities and political troubles in Russia to President Kennedy during the Cuban Missile Crisis in 1962, which helped ease tensions during negotiations between the two powers.

Penkovsky was found out by the KGB (possibly due to their moles in British intelligence, but there is no firm evidence), arrested in October 1962, and executed in 1963. Wynne was arrested, as well, but was sent back to Britain via a spy exchange.

Q: Which nuclear researchers at Los Alamos National Laboratory were actually spies for Russia?

A: Klaus Fuchs was a German physicist who immigrated to Britain when Hitler came to power. He worked on the British atomic project, code-named "Tube Alloy." He was also a communist spy for Russia, and he passed information to the GRU. He was recruited into the US nuclear program at Los Alamos and continued to pass secrets to Russia.

Another Russian spy at Los Alamos was technical assistant and soldier David Greenglass. He was also the brother-in-law of Julius Rosenberg, an electrical engineer, and brother of Ethel Rosenberg (née Ethel Greenglass), who both also worked for the Soviets.

Both Fuchs and Greenglass passed secrets to Russia via a courier named Harry Gold. Fuchs was found out after some of the Venona Decrypts incriminated him, and he gave up Gold, who gave up Greenglass. Greenglass's connection to the Rosenbergs led to their arrest in 1950. The Rosenbergs were put on trial and pleaded innocent.

Several of the group were charged, but to everyone's surprise (including the Russians), the Rosenbergs, and only the Rosenbergs, were sentenced to death. They were given the electric chair in 1953.

Q: Which former senior State Department official and mole for Russia could not be tried for espionage because the statute of limitations had run out?

A: In 1939, Whittaker Chambers, *Time* magazine editor and former agent for Soviet Russia, told Assistant Secretary of State Adolf Berle that State Department official Alger Hiss was a Soviet spy. At the time, Berle didn't believe him. Alger Hiss was a highly regarded US official. Hiss graduated from Johns Hopkins University and Harvard Law, started his State Department service in 1936 as a member of the New Deal Administration, and advised FDR on the building of a new multinational peacekeeping organization, the United Nations (UN), after WWII. In 1947, he became president of the Carnegie Endowment for International Peace.

When Chambers was brought before the House Un-American Activities Committee in 1948, he repeated the accusation against Hiss, who denied it (and denied ever having met Chambers) and sued for libel. But Chambers presented as evidence microfilmed documents (dubbed the "Pumpkin Papers" due to having been hidden in a dried-out pumpkin at his family farm) that incriminated Hiss.

The statute of limitations for espionage had run out, so instead of espionage, they tried Hiss for perjury for lying during the Senate hearings. His first trial ended in a hung jury. But in the second in 1950, Hiss was convicted of perjury and got a sentence of five years. He never admitted his crimes, and some thought him unjustly convicted. In 1996, the Venona Decrypts uncovered more evidence, which disclosed that an American State Department employee who was at Yalta with FDR was an agent for Russia. Hiss was the only one who fit the bill.

Q: Which Beijing opera singer and spy kept a huge secret from their French lover?

A: Shi Pei Pu sang with the Beijing opera, taught Chinese to diplomats, and spoke fluent French. She was also a spy. In 1964, Bernard Boursicot, newly arrived accountant for the French foreign service, met Shi and fell in love with this accomplished and enchanting woman. They had a nearly two-decades-long affair, during which Boursicot passed secrets to Shi for the Chinese government, which he continued to do even after he was transferred away.

Shi told Boursicot that she had been raised as a man, and that she had borne his child, but that the child had been sent away to live with relatives. In 1982, Shi met with Boursicot in Paris, where they were both arrested by French intelligence. They were convicted and jailed in 1986. The papers called Shi the "Chinese Mata Hari."

But Shi had a big secret. She had been born a man, not a woman as she had told Boursicot. When Boursicot found out, he tried to kill himself. The French sent Shi to a men's prison. They were both ultimately pardoned and released.

The story was dramatized in the play *M. Butterfly* by David Henry Hwang.

A : On May 1, 1960, an anti-aircraft weapon near Sverdlovsk Oblast in the Soviet Union shot down a U-2 plane. The pilot, Francis Gary Powers, bailed out, and the KGB arrested him when he landed. They also recovered most of the plane.

Powers was a former Air Force fighter pilot who had started working for the CIA in 1956 when they started flying U-2 spy planes over Soviet airspace. The program surveilled the Soviet Union via the skies to gather intel about their nuclear capabilities.

The CIA, assuming Powers was dead, put out a false story about a weather research plane that had gone down after it malfunctioned and drifted into Soviet airspace. But Russia had the wreckage and could see that it was a spy plane. Russian leader Nikita Khrushchev denounced America for spying on them and lying about it. After President Eisenhower refused to apologize over the incident, Khrushchev backed out of the Paris Summit, during which, among other things, the US and Russia had planned to discuss the easing of tensions between them.

Powers was put on trial in Russia and sentenced to ten years (three in prison and seven at hard labor). But in 1962, Powers and another prisoner were swapped for Soviet spy Rudolf Abel.

Powers wrote a memoir about his ordeal titled *Operation Overflight*, published in 1970. He died in a helicopter crash in 1977.

Q: Which US operation acquired rocket scientists who worked for Hitler's Germany?

A: After the West saw the progress of Hitler's rocket program in the form of the deadly V-1 and V-2 missiles fired at England and in the lead-up to the Cold War against Stalin's Soviet Union, the US sought to get ahold of the scientists who created the projectiles. The US also sought Germany's chemical and biological weapons researchers. At first named Operation Overcast, the recruitment program was redubbed Operation Paperclip. The Joint Intelligence Objectives Agency (JIOA) was created to oversee the operation, and around 1,600 scientists were recruited to work in the US under the program.

President Truman made a rule that the program couldn't recruit Nazi members or supporters, but in some cases, the agency ignored the past records of scientists and even got rid of evidence of their histories in order to hire Nazis. One avid Nazi, Kurt Debus, was made head of the Launch Operations Center at Cape Canaveral in Florida.

The best-known of the group is likely rocket scientist Werner von Braun. He worked on rockets for the US Army and then NASA, and was made director of NASA's Marshall Space Flight Center. He and around 120 other German scientists in the program helped develop the Saturn V rockets used in the *Apollo* moon landing. President Ford considered awarding him the Presidential Medal of Freedom until one of his advisors objected on the basis of von Braun's Nazi history.

Q : Which top-secret nuclear military project racially segregated its scientists and other workers?

A : The Manhattan Project was the top-secret US operation created to develop atomic weapons before Germany. It succeeded, and in August 1945, the US dropped atomic bombs (dubbed Little Boy and Fat Man) on the cities of Hiroshima and Nagasaki in Japan. After witnessing the terrifying devastation of this new weaponry, Japan surrendered.

Despite the name, the project's base of operations was not located in Manhattan. The program was run in three secret cities: Los Alamos, New Mexico; Hanford, Washington; and Oak Ridge, Tennessee. The Oak Ridge location was the largest of the three, housing approximately 75,000 staffers by the end of the war to create fuel for the bombs. The city, which was not on any map, was planned and built by the US Army Corps of Engineers, with housing consisting of single-family homes.

But the Tennessee site also came with built-in racism. Official policies of segregation were still in full swing in the South in the 1940s, so the African American members were housed separately, mostly in something called "hutments," plywood structures with no plumbing that were meant to be temporary, but for some became permanent. The white staffers were much more likely to be moved out of them into real houses.

However, Oak Ridge became one of the first towns in the South to end segregation, probably as a by-product of being settled by scientists and academics.

Incidentally, Russian intelligence knew about the Manhattan Project because of a tip-off from John Cairncross of the Cambridge Five. They dubbed their mission to monitor the operation Project Enormous.

Q: Which now-infamous US senator spurred an anti-communist witch hunt?

A: Senator Joseph McCarthy was convinced that the State Department was overrun with communists. From 1952 to 1954, McCarthy investigated and called witnesses before the Committee on Government Operations of the Senate in an effort to ferret out the supposed communist infiltration of government.

The furor he helped stir up also prompted the House Un-American Activities Committee to go on its own renewed hunt for communists. But it didn't just call State Department officials. It called citizens, including Hollywood writers and actors, many of whom were blacklisted and could no longer find work in Hollywood. On the Senate side, McCarthy called and interrogated US Army officials (and civilians working for the Army) during thirty-six days of televised hearings, after which public opinion turned against him.

The idea that there were Russian spies in the US government wasn't far-fetched, since some had already been caught. But the investigations got out of hand and ensnared and ruined a lot of innocent folk. People started referring to the episode as a "witch hunt." The practice of such an overblown hunt that ends up persecuting the innocent is sometimes also referred to as McCarthyism. Once McCarthy was off the Senate committee, the Senate censured him for his actions.

A: US leaders had a strongly held belief that if one country fell to communism, others around it would follow (the "Domino Theory"). The country of Vietnam (at the time called Indochina, or *Indochine* in French) had been colonized by France in 1887. During WWII, the country was occupied by Japanese forces. Ho Chi Minh (one of the founders of the Indochinese Communist Party), Vo Nguyen Giap, and Pham Van Dong formed a Vietnamese resistance group called the Viet Minh to fight Japan, but they also opposed French rule. After Japan withdrew, Emperor Bao Dai returned to power. But in September 1945, just after WWII, the Viet Minh seized the northern city of Hanoi, and Ho Chi Minh (who was made president of the new northern Vietnamese territory) declared independence from France. Bao Dai stepped down, but France invaded the southern part of the country.

France wanted all of Indochina back and gave new President of the United States Harry Truman a sort of ultimatum: support them in recolonizing Vietnam or get no support from France in any of the US's aims in Europe or against the Soviets. France attacked northern Vietnam in fall 1946 without any objections from the US, and years of skirmishes against the Viet Minh followed. In 1954, France propped up Bao Dai as ruler of southern Vietnam and made Saigon the capital.

In 1950, the US began helping France in earnest by funding and equipping them in their war effort to keep Vietnam from adopting a communist government. But France was losing and suffering major casualties (over 70,000 troops killed and nearly that number injured). They conceded the loss in 1954, and at a meeting of world leaders in Geneva, Switzerland, it was resolved that Ho Chi Minh and his communist government would control the area of

Vietnam north of the 17th Parallel, and Emperor Bao Dai and Prime Minister Ngo Dinh Diem would control the area south of the 17th Parallel until elections scheduled for July 1956 were held to pick leaders for a unified government.

The CIA had intelligence that indicated Ho would likely win if the election were held on schedule, and Vietnam would be under communist rule. So the agency started an operation called the Saigon Military Mission, run by Colonel Edward Lansdale out of the US Embassy in Saigon. The aim was to support Diem and undercut Ho's popularity in the area. Lansdale thwarted more than one coup attempt against Diem and rigged an election in 1955 that resulted in removing Emperor Bao Dai from power, making Diem the sole ruler in South Vietnam.

Teams under Lansdale also worked to sabotage Ho and North Vietnam wherever they could, with missions to contaminate their gas supply, destroy government-controlled printing presses, and sponsor paramilitary groups to infiltrate the area, among other things. One particularly successful mission was Operation Exodus, which spread propaganda that persuaded approximately 1.25 million Catholics in North Vietnam to emigrate to South Vietnam.

The Saigon Military Mission ran from June 1954 to December 1956. The CIA stayed out of affairs in South Vietnam for several years, during which Diem became increasingly dictatorial and a group dubbed the Viet Cong (Vietnamese Communists), with support from North Vietnam, formed, organized, and cultivated a presence in areas all over South Vietnam.

In 1961, the CIA started what they called the Civilian Irregular Defense Groups (CIDG). These groups trained South Vietnamese citizens in combat and defense, and worked at winning them over to the US side with economic and social programs. These CIA-backed local groups (also assisted by the Green Berets) fought the Viet Cong in their local areas.

In 1962, the new Military Assistance Command, Vietnam (MACV) objected to the scope and methods of the CIDG missions. In 1963, Operation Switchback transferred control of the CIDG from the CIA to MACV, and the CIA stepped back into the role of providing intelligence to aid in the conflict.

Q: Which Russian conflict is sometimes referred to as the Soviet Union's "Vietnam?"

A: Russia invaded Afghanistan on December 24, 1979, after a Soviet-backed leader failed to maintain power. They were opposed by a guerilla rebel group called the Mujahideen, one of whose notable leaders was Osama Bin Laden. The US provided arms and other assistance to the Mujahideen, starting a few months before the invasion.

Congressional Representative Charles "Charlie" Wilson of Texas pushed through appropriations to fund the CIAs involvement with the Mujahideen to thwart Russia's plans for the area. Late in the war, the US provided Stinger handheld missiles they used to bring down helicopters and planes. The CIA even transported mules from the US to carry the supplies to the Mujahideen in mountainous areas. Aid to the guerilla fighters totaled around $2 billion.

The conflict wore on until 1989, when the Soviet forces withdrew. The aftermath in some ways led to the worst terrorist attack on US soil. After the war, little effort was made to reconstruct the country, which had been utterly devastated by a decade of war. In 1996, the Taliban took control and enforced strict Islamic rule. And Osama Bin Laden, formerly of the Mujahideen, set to work training members of his group Al-Qaeda, nineteen of whom would carry out the deadly September 11, 2001, attacks on the Twin Towers and the Pentagon.

The book *Charlie Wilson's War* by George Crile III detailed Representative Wilson and other key players' involvement in US aid to the Mujahideen. It was made into a movie in 2007 starring Tom Hanks as the titular character.

Q: Which Cold War spy gave British intelligence secrets in hopes of averting nuclear war?

A: Oleg Gordievsky was a spy for the Soviet Union, stationed at the Soviet embassy in Copenhagen, Denmark. He was upset by his country's actions during the Prague Spring in 1968 under Russian leader Leonid Brezhnev, during which Russia rolled tanks into what was then called Czechoslovakia (now the Czech Republic and Slovakia) and took over to quash the reforms enacted by Alexander Dubček. Gordievsky called his wife about the incident, and the call was overheard by Danish intelligence, who contacted British intelligence agency MI6.

MI6 approached and recruited him in 1974, and Gordievsky passed them information on microfilm until 1978, when he was called back to Moscow. In 1982, he was promoted by the KGB to a post in London, where he resumed contact with MI6. The British gave him unimportant, and sometimes fake, information to pass back to the KGB to keep up appearances that he was doing his job, and he once again passed MI6 information about Russian agents (via once-a-month meetings at a safe house), including names of well-known British politicians.

In the early 1980s, new prime minister Margaret Thatcher in England and new president Ronald Reagan in the United States were including anti-Soviet rhetoric in their speeches. Reagan went so far as to call the Soviet Union the "evil empire" in a 1983 speech and to announce a space-based Strategic Defense Initiative (which never came to pass). By 1982, Russia also had a new leader, Yuri Andropov, former Chairman of the KGB. While he headed the KGB in 1981, the agency initiated an operation called Raketno-Yadernoye Napadenie (RYaN) to monitor for signs of a US nuclear attack. Andropov was convinced that the United States was concocting a plan to launch a nuclear first strike against the USSR.

To further fuel the imaginations of the Soviet government, the North Atlantic Treaty Organization (NATO) ran military exercises dubbed Able Archer in November 1983, which simulated a Western response to a Soviet attack. The exercise, which the Soviets did not know was an exercise, prompted the Soviet government to get its military, including its nuclear weapons, prepared for what they thought was imminent nuclear war.

Gordievsky received a message from the KGB that Operation RYaN had taken on new importance and to watch for signs of any preparation for a nuclear attack. He showed the message to MI6 to convince them that the USSR really believed the West would attack them. The intel was shared with Thatcher and then Reagan. Both softened their anti-Soviet rhetoric, and Reagan met with Soviet Ambassador Anatoly Dobrynin. In 1985, after Andropov and his successor Konstantin Chernenko were succeeded by Mikhail Gorbachev, the USA and the USSR were able to forge a more amicable relationship and ramp down the Cold War tensions.

British intelligence endeavored to keep Gordievsky's status as a mole secret even from the CIA. Eventually, the head of CIA Soviet counterintelligence, Aldrich Ames, guessed the identity of the double agent, in part because he himself was a Russian mole. In 1985, Ames divulged to the KGB the names of all agents providing intel to the CIA. Gordievsky was called back to Russia under false pretenses, where he was tortured, interrogated, and, after failing to confess, put under surveillance and house arrest.

He initiated an escape that had been planned out years earlier. He shook his KGB surveillance, stood in a predetermined place at a certain time, and flashed a British grocery bag to let MI6 agents in Moscow know he needed an exit. To let him know that the message had been received, an MI6 agent walked by him eating a certain brand of chocolate bar. Gordievsky left his family without telling them anything and made his way by train and bus to the Russian border with Finland, where two MI6 agents met him with a car and smuggled him through five checkpoints in the trunk. Gordievsky knew he was safe in Finland when the agents played *Finlandia* by Jean Sibelius to signal him.

Per Gordievsky himself, his escape was the only instance of a Russian agent under heavy surveillance by the KGB successfully fleeing to the West. After the fall of the Soviet Union, he was able to get his family out. And, in 2007, he was awarded Companion of the Most Distinguished Order of St. Michael and St. George by Queen Elizabeth II for his services (incidentally, the same honor given to the fictional agent James Bond).

Q: Which Russian mole planted in the CIA was outed in part by his lavish spending?

A: Aldrich Ames may be the most reviled man in CIA history. His father was with the CIA, and the younger Ames followed in his footsteps, joining the agency in 1962. He specialized in Soviet intelligence and became the CIA's head of Soviet counterintelligence at CIA headquarters in Langley, Virginia.

In April 1985, after more than two decades at the agency, he walked into the Soviet embassy and handed over classified US intelligence. Later in 1985, he handed over the names of all the agents who were providing intel on the Soviet Union, and details of all covert operations that the CIA and FBI were running regarding the Soviets. His actions led to the executions of at least ten spies working for Western intelligence.

He wasn't the only Russian mole ever to penetrate a Western intelligence agency and rise to a lofty position, but Ames did terrible damage by giving up the identities of operatives for the CIA and beyond. In the mid-1980s, when agents for the CIA in Russia were found and executed by the KGB at an alarming rate, the FBI suspected a mole problem, most likely in the CIA. The CIA likewise launched an investigation, at first focusing on possible communication interception or bugging issues, but also considering the possibility of a mole. In 1991, the CIA and FBI together decided to focus solely on finding a mole.

The CIA didn't suspect Ames for a while. Despite screwups at work and an obvious drinking problem, he managed to pass a number of polygraph tests, which were given to agents regularly (but unfortunately are not the most reliable of tests and are easy to trick). He even had regular meetings with his Russian handler, but many were under the guise of recruiting a Soviet agent and therefore easily written off as legitimate CIA business.

Unlike his British compatriots in the Cambridge Five, Ames seemed to be in it for the money. He received around $2.5 million from the KGB and they held around $2.1 million more in a bank in Moscow for him. Ames's lavish spending on new clothing, a red Jaguar, something to the tune of $30,000 in monthly credit card payments, and a house purchased with $540,000 in cash in 1989 caught the attention of investigators. At first it was excused away because his second wife, Rosario, purportedly came from a well-to-do Colombian family. But investigators on the mole-hunting team noticed that on more than one occasion after he'd met with Russians, money was deposited into his bank account. That's when their focus turned to Ames.

The FBI bugged his house, tapped his phone, and got into his computer to gather evidence. Ultimately, they learned that Ames had been a mole for the last nine years of his thirty-year stint at the CIA, and that Rosario had been helping him (one taped conversation was of her reprimanding her husband for his reckless behavior during his missions). The FBI arrested Ames on February 22, 1994, the day before a CIA-sanctioned trip to Russia. He pleaded guilty and received a sentence of life without the possibility of parole. They also arrested Rosario, and she received a sentence of a little over five years and returned to Colombia upon release.

The children and widows of the spies sold out by Ames were later granted American citizenship by Congress. Although the damage he did was incalculable, Ames didn't turn out to be the sole perpetrator of some of the leaks that were initially attributed to him. There was another mole in US intelligence. In fact, in some cases, they were sharing the same data with Russia. Find out who in the next entry.

Q: Who was the highest ranking US intelligence agent to volunteer to pass intel to the Soviet Union?

A: The arrest of Aldrich Ames (a mole for the KGB in the ranks of the CIA) sent shockwaves through US intelligence, as well as great relief that they'd caught the man responsible for the deaths of CIA moles in the Soviet Union (the KGB had them summarily executed when they were found out).

But FBI investigators noticed that something didn't quite add up. There was at least one case that Ames couldn't possibly have known about: that of Felix Bloch. Bloch was a US State Department official placed under surveillance for suspicion of espionage. Just before a meeting in Paris with Russian intelligence, he got a call warning him not to show up. The FBI's investigation was thwarted.

Perhaps that should have been a clue for them to look among their own ranks. But because Ames had been CIA, and maybe also because of occasional rivalry between the two agencies, the FBI still expected to find their mole within the ranks of the CIA.

Robert H. Hanssen, an employee at FBI headquarters in Washington, DC, worked in budgeting but was moved to analytics because of his advanced computing skills. He created a database for the FBI of spies embedded in Russia that FBI agents used to look for links that might point to a culprit.

But unbeknownst to the FBI, Hanssen was the culprit. Hanssen had first offered his services to Soviet military intelligence (the GRU) in 1979. He stopped for a while. Then, in October 1985, Hanssen sent an anonymous letter to Victor Cherkashin, the head of Russian counterintelligence in DC, offering valuable documents, asking for compensation of $100,000, and revealing the identities of two CIA moles in Russia named Martynov and Motorin. The two were shot and killed.

Hanssen appeared to his colleagues to be a devout Catholic family man, and when his wife found out about his spying, he reportedly confessed to a priest and was advised to donate the money he was paid to charity. But he was seeing and helping to support a stripper on the side, and he was recording having sex with his wife, allegedly while a friend in another room watched. And, of course, he continued passing even more highly classified information to the Russians.

He gave his handlers the identities of CIA assets, nuclear and military tech secrets, and the existence of a secret tunnel and listening device that US intelligence had installed underneath the Russian embassy on Mount Alto in Washington, DC.

He used the dead drop method, where he'd place intel in a plastic bag, deposit it at a prearranged spot near his neighborhood for pickup, and leave a piece of tape on a nearby signpost to indicate that he'd made the drop. He never had to meet his handlers in person. In fact, he never revealed his true identity to them at all. He communicated with them using the alias "Ramon Garcia" the whole time he worked for Russia. They even mistakenly believed him to be in the CIA, notably because "Garcia" ends in "cia."

In 1993, Hanssen hacked into the FBI mainframe and accessed data on operations in the Russia section. When his breach was caught, he convinced his superiors that he had done it to test their computer system's security. The bureau let it go, and he continued tapping into FBI systems. For a while the FBI thought they might be leaking data due to a communications or codes breach rather than a human double agent.

They settled on a new suspect as Graysuit (their code name for the unknown mole), a CIA agent named Brian Kelley. Kelley had been involved in the Bloch case, and happened to live near Hanssen. They kept Kelley under constant surveillance, and at one point found a map on his kitchen table they thought was to his drop site. It was a map of his jogging route.

The FBI caught a lucky break in 2000 when a Russian agent approached and offered them a file on the asset known as Ramon Garcia. He asked for $7 million, and they paid it. The file didn't have the mole's real name, but it did include one of the plastic bags used for a drop and a recording of a conversation between Garcia and a Russian handler. The investigators expected to hear Kelley's voice, but instead, they heard Hanssen's.

The team wanted more evidence, so they surveilled Hanssen. They transferred Hanssen to a job overseeing FBI computer security and assigned him an aid, Eric O'Neill. O'Neill was computer-savvy like Hanssen, but he was also a ghost assigned to closely monitor Hanssen. O'Neill noticed that Hanssen was very protective of his Palm Pilot, a pre-smartphone electronic personal digital assistant (PDA). The FBI summoned Hanssen to the firing range for an unscheduled shooting assessment, something he hated doing, to hopefully provoke him into making a mistake. He grabbed his gun and went to the firing range in the basement. O'Neill entered his office and found that Hanssen had, indeed, left his Palm Pilot in his briefcase. He ran it to a team waiting with equipment to hack it. When he got a page that Hanssen was on his way back, he rushed it back to Hanssen's office and put it back in the briefcase. By his own account, O'Neill made the rookie mistake of forgetting which briefcase pocket he took it out of and had to hope for the best.

The FBI got information from the PDA on Hanssen's next scheduled drop, which was actually to be his last drop, scheduled for February 18, 2001, at Foxstone Park in nearby Vienna, Virginia. They were expecting the drop to be under a footbridge at 7 p.m., but the place and time had been moved unbeknownst to the agents. Hanssen did show up at Foxstone Park, but shortly after the FBI had set up around the footbridge, closer to 4 p.m., Hanssen bypassed the bridge and walked into the woods. They didn't see the actual drop, but had a SWAT team grab him on his way home.

Upon arrest, Hanssen reportedly said, "What took you so long?" He confessed everything, and it turned out he had done even more damage than originally thought. When news of his arrest and activities broke to the rest of the bureau, they were shocked. Someone in their own ranks had been undoing much of their work behind their backs. People were reportedly crying in the office.

Like Ames, Hanssen received life in prison—fifteen consecutive life sentences. Unlike Ames's looser accommodations, Hanssen was placed in solitary confinement in a supermax prison in Colorado.

Hanssen mentioned that he was inspired to become a double agent when he read Kim Philby's autobiography, *My Silent War*.

Q: Which covert operation inadvertently led to the shooting down of a civilian airplane?

A: On September 1, 1983, the Soviet military shot down Korean Airlines flight 007, killing 269 people. After what appeared to be a blatant act of aggression on the Soviet Union's part, US President Ronald Reagan escalated his anti-Soviet rhetoric. Tensions between the US and Russia were at an all-time high during this time, and the US reportedly teetered on the brink of war.

What Reagan and even intelligence officials did not know was that the US was conducting highly classified flights to test the Soviet air borders. Soviet intelligence mistook the South Korean flight for one of America's secret flight missions. This terrible loss of life was likely the unintended consequence of a Cold War covert operation against an adversary who at the time believed the US was gearing up to attack them.

A : The peace of a quiet suburban neighborhood in Montclair, New Jersey, was temporarily shattered on June 27, 2010, when the feds swept in to arrest Vladimir and Lydia Guryev, who had been known to their neighbors for over a decade as Richard and Cynthia Murphy.

It turned out that the Guryevs were deep-cover Russian foreign intelligence service, or SVR, agents living under false identities. Their neighbors had no inkling. And their own daughters, born in the US, didn't know either!

The Guryevs had trained at Russian intelligence's institute and worked for Directorate S in the SVR. They were married by order of their agency and sent to the US as illegals, meaning agents who come into the country under false pretenses and have no diplomatic cover.

The couple had been tasked with joining groups to befriend influential people and gather intelligence for Russia. And they weren't alone. Other agents in the ring were scattered across the US in well-off neighborhoods.

Colonel Alexander Potayev of the SVR disclosed their identities to the CIA, along with eight other agents in the same spy ring: Andrey Bezrukov (aka Donald Howard Heathfield), Anna Chapman (aka Anna Kushinko), Mikhail Kutsik (aka Michael Zottoli), Vicky Palaez, Natalia Pereverzeva (aka Patricia Mills), Mikhail Semenko, Mikhail Vasenkov (aka Juan Lazaro), and Elena Vavilova (aka Tracey Lee Ann Foley). An FBI counterintelligence unit set to work investigating the ring under the code name Operation Ghost Stories.

All ten sleeper agents were put under heavy surveillance. They were using common spy techniques like brush passes, dead drops, and coded online messages. Cynthia Murphy was found to have been cozying up to Alan Patricof, possibly to get closer to Hillary Clinton, with whom he had connections.

One of the ring members, Anna Chapman (Kushinko), lived on her own and, unlike the others, wasn't hiding the fact that she was Russian. She had a handler named Roman, but the FBI tricked her into meeting an undercover agent claiming to be her new handler.

CIA director Leon Panetta raised the issue with President Obama of getting Potayev out of Moscow for his safety. The president was soon to meet with Russian Prime Minister Dmitry Medvedev, so they decided to arrest the entire ring when Medvedev was on his way back to Russia. Potayev had to leave Moscow and get to the Ukraine, then to Frankfurt, on his own, from where he was flown to the US. The entire group was arrested after Medvedev left for Moscow, as planned.

Panetta suggested a spy swap to Mikhail Fradkov, head of the SVR. Russia offered four agents for the ten. The Americans chose Alexander Zaporozhsky (the agent who helped catch Ames and Hanson), Gennady Vasilenko, and Igor Sutyagin, and asked MI6 to name the fourth. They chose Sergei Skripal, a former double agent of theirs. The two organizations carried out the swap at an airport in Vienna, Austria.

The children, although citizens by birth, were also eventually repatriated to Russia to be with their parents.

The bizarre story of the sleeper ring inspired the spy show *The Americans* on the FX network.

A: This actually happened more than once. On September 7, 1978, in London, Bulgarian dissident Georgi Markov was stabbed in the thigh with the end of an umbrella. He thought it was an accident, but he died a few days later. The autopsy revealed that a small pellet filled with ricin was lodged in Markov's thigh, likely injected by the assassin's umbrella.

Nearly forty years later, in March 2018, Sergei Skripal and his visiting daughter Yulia were poisoned in Salisbury, England. Skripal and his daughter were found unconscious on a bench. Skripal had been pardoned by the previous Russian administration, but someone poisoned him with the very distinctive Russian nerve agent Novichok.

Two Russian men who were in the area are suspected of possibly putting the nerve agent on the doorknob of the Skripal home. As a result of the poisoning, the UK expelled twenty-three Russian diplomats.

After the initial attack, other victims emerged, including Detective Sergeant Nick Baily and another unidentified Metropolitan police officer, both exposed while investigating the crime. Later in June 2018, Dawn Sturgess and her partner Charlie Rowley were exposed, possibly from a bottle discarded by the poisoners. Sturgess died, but all the other victims, including the Skripals, recovered.

Q : Who was the first person we know to have been assassinated with radiation?

A : Alexander Litvinenko served in the Russian military, and then the KGB and the Federal Security Service (FSB). At the FSB, he investigated internal corruption in the agency. In 1998, he claimed he was ordered to kill Russian political opponents. He was fired and arrested. In 2000, he went to England and asked for asylum. He became a British citizen in 2006.

Litvinenko cowrote a book titled *Blowing up Russia: Terror from Within*, in which he alleged that the FSB had orchestrated apartment bombings in 1999 that were blamed on Chechnya, and that Russia had killed journalist Anna Politkovskaya, who wrote critically of the war with Chechnya.

In November 2006, Litvinenko took tea with former Russian agents Andrei Lugovoi and Dmitri Kovtun at a London hotel. Litvinenko became ill shortly thereafter. He died weeks later, and it was discovered that the cause was polonium-210 poisoning, possibly slipped into his tea. Polonium-210 isn't very dangerous to us outside the body. It can easily be washed off and doesn't emit radiation that penetrates human skin. But if it enters the body through ingestion, inhalation, or an open wound, it causes organ damage from emission of alpha particles due to the radioactive decay of the substance, which tends to settle in the kidneys, liver, and spleen. Symptoms may include nausea, vomiting, diarrhea, severe headaches, loss of hair, and, if enough is present, death.

Litvinenko believed it was the Kremlin that had him poisoned, but the truth was never uncovered. He was reportedly looking into Russian mafia links in Spain at the time of his death.

CHAPTER 8

THE BEST-LAID PLANS
FAMOUS FOIBLES AND FAILURES

Q: Which conspirator in a failed covert operation to blow up British Parliament has a holiday named after him?

A: By the time of the Gunpowder Plot, England had a long and storied history of tension between Protestants and Catholics. It began around 1533 when Henry VIII wanted a divorce, forbidden under Catholicism, and started the Protestant Church of England. His young successor, King Edward VI, continued his anti-Catholic policies. Edward's successor, (his sister) Mary I, who was still a Catholic, began putting Protestants to death for heresy, earning her the nickname Bloody Mary. She was succeeded by her sister Elizabeth, a protestant, who made Catholic mass illegal again and instituted fines for people who didn't attend the Church of England. After Pope Pius V excommunicated Elizabeth I from the Catholic church via a papal bull that suggested her subjects should defy her, she banned priests from England, made sheltering them an act of treason, and had many priests put to death.

In 1603, James VI of Scotland (son of Mary, Queen of Scots) became King James I of England. He declared Scotland and England united, and at first relaxed the fines on recusants (English people who remained Catholic), but he later reinstated the fees to raise revenue and spoke out against Catholicism.

In this setting, a group of five Catholic noblemen, led by Robert Catesby, hatched a terrorist plot against the English government. They met in 1604 at a Catholic refuge, the Duck and Drake Inn. They included Catesby, John Wright, Thomas Percy, Thomas Wintour, and Guido Fawkes (later known as Guy Fawkes).

Catesby's plan was to blow up Westminster Palace during the opening of Parliament, at which King James I and other members of the monarchy would be present. They decided at some point that James's daughter Elizabeth should be crowned monarch after James's death in the explosion, and would be given Catholic guardians and reeducated into Catholicism. Parliament's opening was postponed until November 5, 1605 (the following year), due to plague, which gave them lots of time to plan, but also lots of time to be found out.

Fawkes, a Spanish soldier, had been recruited by John Wright, an old schoolmate, because they needed someone who knew how to use gunpowder. Later, others joined the plot, including Robert Wintour (Thomas's brother), Christopher Wright (John's brother), Robert Keyes, John Grant, Sir Everard Digby, Francis Tresham, Thomas Bates (Catesby's servant), and Ambrose Rookwood. Rookwood was, in fact, not told of the plot right away and thought he was acquiring gunpowder to send to Catholic soldiers in Flanders.

Percy rented a house adjacent to the House of Lords, and Fawkes stayed at the residence undercover as Percy's servant "John Johnson." The men gradually smuggled gunpowder into the cellar until they amassed thirty-six barrels.

Shortly before the planned event, someone sent an anonymous letter to William Parker (aka Lord Monteagle). It said not to attend the November 5 opening of Parliament, warned of a terrible blow, and said to burn the letter. Many think it was sent by Tresham, who tried to talk Catesby out of the plot at some point, and who happened to be Monteagle's brother-in-law.

Monteagle showed the note to a few members of the House of Lords and to Secretary of State Robert Cecil. They decided to consult the king when he got back from a hunting trip. Monteagle's servant, Thomas Ward, related to the Wrights by marriage, told Catesby about the letter. Most of the group wanted to abort the plan, but Catesby convinced them to go forward.

King James ordered a search of the properties around Westminster. They found Fawkes guarding a cellar full of firewood, but didn't search underneath the wood, where the gunpowder was. When King James was told of the cellar, he ordered a second search, during which they found the gunpowder and arrested Fawkes. After news of the foiled plot spread, people all over the country lit bonfires in celebration.

King James's men discovered the fact that Thomas Percy leased the house. Sir John Popham, the Lord Chief Justice, used a network of informants among the Catholics to come up with names of likely conspirators. From this intel, Catesby, Percy, Rookwood, Grant, Tom Wintour, the Wrights, and Thomas Bates (as his alias Robert Ashfield) were proclaimed traitors and their arrests ordered.

The authorities didn't know about Tresham, Keyes, Digby, or Robert Wintour yet. At first, Guy Fawkes resisted giving up the conspirators. But he cracked under torture on November 7 and revealed all of their names.

The would-be assassins had arranged to meet at Dunchurch (where they planned to abduct the young Elizabeth for the next phase of their plan). Catesby and several of the plotters headed out before Fawkes's arrest. The rest fled to meet them when they learned of the failure. Catesby hoped to raise an army but only managed to enlist the help of Stephen Littleton and Henry Morgan.

Robert Keyes fled, and the rest rode to Littleton's home in Staffordshire, stealing supplies (including gunpowder) on the way. The gunpowder got wet, and they decided to dry it out a little too close to the fire. It exploded, blinding Grant and injuring two others. Digby, Robert Wintour, Bates, and Littleton left. The rest remained. On November 8, the sheriff of Worcestershire led two hundred men to arrest the failed terrorists. A gunfight ensued, and most of the group was wounded. Catesby, Percy, and the two Wrights died of their wounds. Bates, Keyes, and Digby were captured.

On November 9, King James gave a speech, perhaps to avoid inspiring more assassination plots, stating the idea that many Catholics were misguided but loyal subjects. Parliament declared that every November 5, the English would attend a service celebrating the king's escape.

Eventually, the remaining plotters were captured. Tresham died of an illness before the trial. They all signed confessions, but during the trial on January 27, 1606, all but Digby pleaded not guilty. They were, however, all found guilty. The sentence was gruesome: they were to be hung, cut down before death, have some of their bits cut off, and then drawn and quartered. Guy Fawkes was put to death last. His neck broke during the hanging, so he was spared the more grizzly stages of his punishment.

The November 5 service went on until 1859, but the annual celebration continues to this day. In the 1700s, Guy Fawkes became the focus (despite all the other plotters and the fact that he was not the ringleader). Aside from the traditional bonfires, people started burning his effigy, a practice called "burning the Guy."

The Guy Fawkes mask, an artistic rendering of Guy Fawkes himself, is now also used as a symbol for flouting authority. The title character, V, in Alan Moore and David Lloyd's comic *V for Vendetta*, donned the mask as he fought against a totalitarian British government (and, indeed, carried out a version of the original plot). And the mask is used as a symbol for the cyber hacking group (or loose collective) Anonymous. Incidentally, his name is also where the word "guy," meaning any man, originated.

Q: Which French military officer was famously railroaded for an offense he didn't commit?

A: Captain Alfred Dreyfus, a 35-year-old captain in the French Army, fell victim to what is often referred to as "The Dreyfus Affair." In 1894, a cleaning woman at the German embassy, who was really working for French counterintelligence, found a letter regarding French military plans in the wastepaper basket of a German attaché.

Dreyfus was court-martialed and convicted of being the culprit of leaking the information, despite the fact that the handwriting didn't match his own. Dreyfus was Jewish, and anti-Semitism abounded, which likely played a role in his wrongful conviction. His conviction was even used to ramp up fears of Jewish conspiracies. Dreyfus was given a life sentence on Devil's Island in French Guiana.

A new chief of Army intelligence, Lieutenant Colonel Georges Picquart, despite himself being an anti-Semite, believed the evidence pointed to Major Ferdinand Walsin Esterhazy, a Christian with friends in high places. Esterhazy was acquitted, and Picquart was transferred to Africa.

Opinions on the affair divided the nation. Famous French author Emile Zola even got caught up in the drama. Zola wrote a newspaper article titled "J'accuse!" (or "I accuse!"), lambasting the French military for prejudice. The government accused him of libel. He was convicted and sentenced to imprisonment but managed to escape to England.

In 1906, the new French president granted Dreyfus a pardon. He returned to service in the French Army for a year before retiring, then rejoined to fight for his country during World War I, despite his ill treatment.

Q: What clever ruse by a British SOE radio operator tricked a German agent into revealing their allegiance?

A: During WWII, a British SOE radio operator was receiving transmissions in Morse code that were supposedly from one of their own agents in the Netherlands. But the operator noticed something odd about the messages. They weren't typical of what the agent in question usually sent.

The transmissions were being sent by a German operator assuming the identity of an SOE agent. In a clever ruse, Leo Marks sent a message back with the sign-off HH (short for "heil Hitler"). The German sender, by force of habit, replied HH back, revealing his or her identity as a Nazi spy.

Q: What capture of an SOE agent led to the capture of over fifty more?

A: On March 6, 1942, the German military intelligence agency Abwehr captured Hubertus Lauwers, a Dutch SOE agent, when he was sent back into Holland. The Nazis made him transmit requests to the SOE for more agents and supplies.

He tried to signal that he was captured by leaving out his bluff check and starting one message with "cau" and ending it with "ght," but the receivers didn't catch the code. Leo Marks noticed the missing check but was told by SOE's Dutch unit that they had looked into it and the agent was fine.

His forced transmissions went on for nearly a year. The SOE sent more agents, over fifty of whom were captured. Most of them were executed. Only Lauwers and three other agents survived.

Q: What ill-conceived attempt at psychological warfare involved fake postage stamps?

A: During WWII, the newly created American intelligence service, the Office of Strategic Services (OSS), hatched a plan they dubbed "Operation Cornflakes." They made parodies of German postage stamps and got them into Germany in hopes of sowing discord and demoralizing the enemy.

One stamp showed Hitler with part of his skull exposed and the normal motto *Deutsches Reich* (German empire) replaced with *Futsches Reich* (something like "ruined empire"). It's doubtful they did much to alter the course of the war.

Q: What covert operation to spy on Soviet leader Nikita Khrushchev ended in decapitation?

A: In 1956, Nikita Khrushchev paid an official state visit to England aboard the Russian naval vessel *Ordzhonikidze*, a brand-new high-tech cruiser. MI6 sent Buster Crabb, an officer in the British Navy, on a mission to dive underneath the new vessel and gather intelligence, especially on the propeller.

A few days later, his headless body washed up on a beach at Chichester Harbour. Sir John Alexander Sinclair, head of MI6, claimed at a hearing on the incident that Crabb was on a period of absence and there was no evidence that the body was Crabb's. He expressed outrage at the accusation that MI6 would spy on a visiting foreign leader. He was dismissed as head of the agency.

Q: What plot by the CIA to foment revolt in Cuba failed famously?

A: Fidel Castro became leader of Cuba in 1959 after the overthrow of Fulgencio Batista. He steered the country toward communism and allied it with Russia. During the Cold War, when the US was making a concerted effort to stop the spread of communism, the government started working on a plan to depose Castro.

The planning phase started during the Eisenhower administration, but the actual attempt wasn't made until after the election of President John F. Kennedy, who took office in January 1961.

For whatever reason, the CIA left their analytical staff out of the planning process. And the CIA's Deputy Director of Plans at the time, Richard Bissell, who was in charge of the mission, had little experience working with spies.

In April 1961, the US dropped off over a thousand Cuban exiles at the Bay of Pigs in Cuba. The hope was that they would be able to start a revolt against Castro. But the group was attacked immediately by Castro's forces. Because the involvement of the Americans was supposed to be a secret (under the concept of "plausible deniability"), the exiled troops had no support, and they were captured. The embarrassing failure led to Allen Dulles's removal as director of the CIA and more oversight of the agency.

This wasn't the only attempt to oust Castro. There were others either meant to foment revolt or to flat-out assassinate him. But they all failed, perhaps in part because each one of the thirty-eight agents recruited in Cuba by the CIA had been turned by Cuban intelligence agency Dirección General de Inteligencia. They were all feeding disinformation back to the US. Fidel Castro remained in power until 2008 and lived to the ripe old age of 90.

Q: What faulty intel was used as an excuse to invade Iraq?

A: Intelligence agencies believed that Iraq (under its leader, Saddam Hussein) was working on weapons of mass destruction (WMDs), including biological, chemical, and nuclear weapons. After the first Gulf War in 1991, Iraq had chemical and biological weapons programs and was trying to develop nuclear weapons capabilities. These programs were stopped, but the UN had issues inspecting to make sure they were really over.

The US was also undertaking a new "war on terror" in the aftermath of the devastating surprise attacks on the World Trade Center and the Pentagon on September 11, 2001 (often referred to as 9/11).

President George W. Bush (son of former president George H. W. Bush, president during the first Gulf War) and British Prime Minister Tony Blair decided to take action in Iraq due to a reported threat of WMDs. The two powers invaded the country in March 2003. Hussein lost and was ousted very quickly. But no WMD programs were found.

The evidence used to justify the attacks was scant and sometimes conflicting. For instance, Italian intelligence had a document showing that Iraq bought yellowcake uranium in Niger, but that document turned out to be forged, and there was no other confirming evidence. George Tenet, director of the CIA, had warned officials against using that bit of intel, but the president brought it up in a speech. And the Bush administration leaked to the press that Iraq had purchased aluminum tubes for their nuclear program, but the Energy Department (in charge of the US nuclear programs) believed they were more likely for rockets.

Administration officials also mentioned a meeting between one of the Al Qaeda 9/11 hijackers and Iraqi intelligence that was alleged by a foreign government, but the US Intelligence Community couldn't substantiate the claim.

Further controversy ensued when the world found out about secret CIA prisons (or "black sites") in various parts of the world. The CIA flew terrorism suspects to these prisons and used interrogation techniques that are classified by most countries as torture.

The US learned after the invasion that Iraq's nuclear program ended in 1991, its chemical weapons program likely ended in 1991, and its biological weapons research ended in 1996.

Q: Which country's embassy in the Balkans did NATO destroy due to bad map intel?

A: During the genocide being perpetrated by Serbian President Slobodan Milosevic against Albanians in Kosovo, NATO bombed Serbia to try to make them stop. In 1999, NATO forces destroyed a building in downtown Belgrade. They thought this building housed the Yugoslav Federal Directorate for Supply and Procurement (FDSP), an agency dealing with military equipment.

Unfortunately, the building was actually the Chinese embassy. The FDSP was down the street from it, around 383 yards away. The CIA had provided incorrect location information, apparently due to an outdated map. Three journalists at the embassy were killed. Two were newlyweds Xu Xinghu and Zhu Ying, and the other was Shao Yunhuan, whose husband was blinded in the attack. Around twenty were injured. Military attaché Ren Baokai was in a coma, from which he later recovered. And one bomb fell through the roof of ambassador Pan Zhanlin's home next to the embassy, but thankfully it was a dud and the ambassador survived.

The incident sparked outrage in China, and protests raged outside the US and British embassies for days. Many believed it was an intentional act by the US. The US paid $28 million to China for embassy damage and $4.5 million to the families of those killed or wounded in the bombing.

Q: What feathered scientific subject was falsely accused of being a spy?

A: A vulture dubbed R65 was captured and held in Saudi Arabia in 2011. The GPS transmitter it was carrying was marked with Hebrew letters, which raised suspicion that the bird was being used to spy for Mossad, the national intelligence agency of Israel. It turned out to be part of a Tel Aviv University study of vulture migratory patterns. Prince Bandar bin Saud Al Saud cleared the vulture of charges and ordered its release.

In December 2010, there was a similar incident when Mohamed Abdul Fadil Shousha, regional governor of South Sinai in Egypt, repeated a conspiracy theory that sharks that attacked five people over six days in a resort area on the Red Sea may have been released by Israeli intelligence. The suspects, two whitetip sharks, were caught and killed, but a conservation group concluded they weren't necessarily the culprits.

CHAPTER 9

SPY AGENCIES

PAST AND PRESENT

Q : What prompted the creation of the US Secret Service?

A : The US Secret Service was created in 1865, the same year President Abraham Lincoln was assassinated, which would lead one to believe it was created to protect the president. But that's not actually the case. The Secret Service was originally formed to combat the threat of counterfeit money, which flooded the country near the end of the Civil War. That's why the agency was placed within the Department of the Treasury.

After the assassination of President William McKinley in 1901, the agency broadened its scope to include protecting the president of the United States and other US leaders, their families, visiting foreign leaders, and occasionally, large events.

In March 2003, the Secret Services was removed from the Treasury Department and placed within the Department of Homeland Security.

Q: What US cryptology agency cracked Japan's version of the Enigma machine?

A: In 1929, US Secretary of State Henry Stimson shuttered the State Department's cryptology division, expressing his preference for diplomacy over espionage by saying, "Gentlemen do not read each other's mail." The comment may have been aimed at Herbert Yardley, who worked during WWI in the US Department of State's "Black Chamber," which broke the Japanese naval codes.

But intelligence was still necessary for some purposes, so the Army created the Signal Intelligence Service (SIS) in April 1930. William F. Friedman, who was charged with leading the department, had actually worked with Yardley during WWI. Friedman coined the term "cryptanalysis."

In 1939, Japan developed a new and improved version of the German Enigma machine, which they called Alphabetical Typewriter 97. The SIS focused entirely on breaking this machine's code. The effort was called Operation Magic, and Friedman called his team of cryptologists magicians. They also referred to the decrypted messages as magic.

The group examined the beginnings and endings of messages for common greetings and sign-offs, which proved fruitful because of diplomatic formalities, and crunched numbers to find patterns. The department succeeded in building a copy of the Japanese machine that they dubbed "Purple," and which was able to successfully decrypt Japanese communications.

At one point, they deciphered messages that indicated Japanese Admiral Isoroku Yamamoto was planning a major attack at a location called AF, but the Allies had no idea where that location was. Some thought it might be the Midway Atoll, where the US had a base, but they needed confirmation. The base at Midway

Atoll was ordered to send a message to Pearl Harbor that their evaporators had broken down and they were running low on fresh water.

SIS then decrypted messages from Japan about AF's water problem, revealing that their big plans were, indeed, for an attack on Midway Atoll. On June 4, 1942, Japan attacked Midway, but American forces were ready and defeated them.

Q: Who ran the FBI for nearly fifty years?

A: The beginnings of the FBI came about in 1908, when the Department of Justice expanded Chief Examiner Stanley W. Finch's office by hiring ten former Secret Service officers. In 1909, the department was renamed the Bureau of Investigation, and in 1935, the Federal Bureau of Investigation. Its initial aim was to target criminals who crossed state lines.

J. Edgar Hoover joined the Bureau of Investigation in 1917. In 1919, Attorney General A. Mitchell Palmer put Hoover in charge of a group dedicated to collecting intel on leftist radical groups after a spate of bombings attributed to anarchists. The Bureau of Investigation was in the process of conducting the infamous Palmer Raids, where thousands of suspected "radicals" (including members of trade unions) were rounded up, often without due process, subjected to beatings and other abuses, and sometimes deported. Most of the arrests and deportations were reversed, and the raids ended in 1920.

Hoover became acting director of the FBI in 1924. He expanded the agency and spent the 1930s fighting organized crime. After WWII, he once again focused the agency on communist organizations and other groups he considered subversive, and he cooperated with the House Un-American Activities Committee. From 1956 to 1971, he ran an operation called COINTELPRO (short for Counter Intelligence Program) that surveilled, infiltrated, and disrupted the activities of hate groups, communist and socialist organizations, civil rights groups, and antiwar groups (see the COINTELPRO entry in Chapter 11 for more detail).

Revelations of the program's extreme activities against citizens marred the reputation of the FBI, and along with Watergate abuses, led to greater oversight of the agency, including stipulations that the head of the FBI can only serve ten years and that the position requires Senate confirmation.

Hoover's tenure as head of the FBI ran from May 10, 1924 to May 2, 1972 (the date of his death), just shy of forty-eight years.

Q: What organization did Winston Churchill create to sow dissent behind enemy lines?

A: After the fall of France to Germany in 1940, Churchill hatched a plan to foment resistance in territories occupied by Axis powers. He created a new organization called the Special Operations Executive (SOE). The agency sent spies all over the world to foment resistance, funnel supplies to resistance groups, and commit acts of sabotage to Axis powers within occupied countries. The agency had around 13,000 employees at its peak.

Q: Which WWII-era British intelligence agency's name was a pun?

A: Set up in January 1941, Britain's Twenty Committee was tasked with capturing German spies and trying to get them to work for the Allies instead. Germany sent around 170 spies into Britain over the course of the war. The Twenty Committee managed the remarkable feat of capturing most of them and turning dozens into double agents.

Near the end of the war, Germany launched new V-1 and V-2 missiles at England (the "V" stood for *Vergeltungswaffen,* German for "vengeance weapon"). The V-1 was essentially the first cruise missile, and the V-2 the first long-range ballistic missile. These long-range weapons flew further and faster than any weapons created before and wrought terrible carnage. Germany launched over twenty thousand V-1s, mostly at England, and three thousand V-2s.

Thankfully, they weren't terribly accurate, in part due to the Twenty Committee, which used fake Nazi agents to sow misinformation that made Germany believe they had struck places other than where they had actually hit. Their deception caused the Nazis to recalibrate and inadvertently divert the missiles toward less heavily populated areas, although the missiles still killed thousands of people.

The business of the Twenty Committee was serious, but their name was a sort of joke. The Roman numeral for twenty is "XX." Those letters could also be referred to as a "double cross," which is the job of a counterintelligence agency—to double-cross the enemy.

Q: What was the first official United States intelligence service that operated worldwide?

A: As a result of the intelligence failure that led to the US missing signs of the impending attack at Pearl Harbor that occurred December 7, 1941, the government created a new counterintelligence agency to help thwart the Axis powers' plans. In July 1941, President Franklin Delano Roosevelt appointed William J. "Wild Bill" Donovan (a lawyer and decorated WWI hero) to the post of Coordinator of Information (COI). His office reported intel directly to the president. In June 1942, the COI office became the Office of Strategic Services (OSS). Its role was similar to that of Churchill's Special Operations Executive (SOE). The agency had around ten thousand agents, some of whom became heads of a future agency, the CIA.

J. Edgar Hoover wanted his FBI to be in charge of wartime counterintelligence, leading to some clashes between the FBI and OSS.

President Harry Truman shut the OSS down shortly after the war on September 20, 1945.

A : The National Security Act of September 1947 created three new governmental bodies to conduct counterintelligence against Russia intelligence. They were the Department of Defense, the National Security Council (NSC), and the Central Intelligence Agency (CIA).

The aim of the CIA (sometimes referred to as "The Company") was to gather intelligence and inform the US government on threats from foreign powers. A policy directive signed by Truman in April 1950, the NSC-68, defined the role of the CIA as including espionage, intelligence gathering, covert ops, psychological warfare, and paramilitary operations.

The director of the CIA was in charge of all intelligence collection for the United States, even by other government agencies. Many former OSS staffers were hired to work for the CIA.

Q: Which body acted as the Shah of Iran's secret police?

A: The last Shah of Iran, Mohammad Reza Pahlavi, was supported by the United States.

The Shah had his secret police organization, the Savak (an abbreviation of the Farsi for "Security and Intelligence Organization"), surveil the populace of Iran and even Iranian students who were studying abroad. He was known for committing human rights violations in the process of quashing dissent.

The CIA worked with the Savak because Iran was a good spot to listen in on Russian radio communications.

The Savak was disbanded in 1979 after the Iranian Revolution led by the Ayatollah Khomeini. The revolt caught the US by surprise because the CIA was getting their intel on Iran from the Savak, which didn't see it coming, either.

Q: Which British organization operating in the US was tasked with helping get the US into WWII?

A: The office of British Security Coordination (BSC) was headquartered in New York and, to an extent, had the backing of the FBI under J. Edgar Hoover. The office, headed by Sir William Stephenson, was tasked with getting the US into WWII, and it often went beyond what the FBI sanctioned in its efforts to do so. The organization did things like plant stories in US newspapers favorable to Britain, thwart businesses of Axis powers in the US, and reveal, and sometimes sabotage, the shipment of instruments of war from the US to Germany. The agency made efforts to counter the America First isolationist groups who wanted to keep the US out of the war.

Q: Which US president was formerly head of the CIA?

A: President George Herbert Walker Bush, elected in 1988, was sometimes characterized as a wimp by opponents. But in 1976, before his presidency, he was made head of the CIA. He had to deal with the aftermath left by revelations of CIA misdeeds that followed the Watergate scandal. So far, he is the only CIA head to become president of the United States.

Q: Which super-secret US intelligence agency is jokingly said to stand for "No Such Agency?"

A: In 1952, President Harry Truman created a new intelligence branch called the National Security Agency (NSA) by signing a classified memorandum. The agency was tasked with monitoring signals intelligence, which means they monitor both electronic communications and nonverbal signals produced by electronic means, such as radar signals. The existence of the NSA was supposed to be secret. Its existence was hidden, even from Congress.

By the late 1960s, it became the largest US intelligence agency, with over ninety thousand employees (although its numbers have dwindled somewhat over the years). It was thrown into the public eye during the 1975 investigation by the US Senate's Select Committee to Study Government Operations with Respect to Intelligence Activities (aka the Church Committee) after the Watergate scandal.

Q: How many intelligence agencies does the US have?

A: At the time of this writing, the US has seventeen government intelligence agencies in its Intelligence Community (IC). This may seem like overkill, but they all have slightly different missions, as follows:

- **Office of the Director of National Intelligence (ODNI):** This independent agency is tasked with overseeing all other agencies in the IC (foreign, domestic, and military intelligence agencies), and acting as advisor on intelligence matters to the president of the United States (POTUS), the National Security Council (NSC), and the Homeland Security Council.

- **Central Intelligence Agency (CIA):** Another independent agency (except that it is under the ODNI), the CIA gathers and analyzes intelligence related to national security and provides related information to US government officials.

- **Department of Energy Office of Intelligence and Counter-intelligence (OICI):** In the effort to protect technologies and information (including nuclear secrets) and advise the US government in matters related to energy security, this agency oversees all intelligence activities within the Department of Energy.

- **Department of Homeland Security Office of Intelligence and Analysis (I&A):** This agency collects intelligence from various sources and analyzes it to assess possible threats to the US.

- **Department of State Bureau of Intelligence and Research (INR):** This entity provides intelligence and analysis related to US foreign policy to the US secretary of state.

- **Department of Treasury Office of Intelligence and Analysis (OIA):** This agency receives, analyzes, and disseminates intelligence related to financial systems, both to safeguard US financial systems and to counter terrorists, drug cartels, terrorist groups, rogue nations, and similar threats.

- **Drug Enforcement Administration Office of National Security Intelligence (ONSI):** Under the DEA, which is under the Department of Justice, this agency coordinates intelligence gathering and sharing with other IC agencies related to combating drug running and global terrorism.

- **Federal Bureau of Investigation (FBI):** Under the Department of Justice, the FBI undertakes intelligence and law-enforcement activities, including infiltrating groups that mean to harm the US.

- **US Coast Guard Intelligence (CGI):** Now part of the Department of Homeland Security, this agency provides intelligence related to all things maritime, including safety on the waters, national security threats from the waters, and protection of the sea.

- **Defense Intelligence Agency (DIA):** Under the Department of Defense (DOD), this agency gathers and manages foreign military intelligence and directly advises the Secretary of Defense and the chairman of the Joint Chiefs of Staff.

- **National Geospatial-Intelligence Agency (NGA):** Under the Department of Defense, the NGA provides geospatial intelligence to civilian and military groups to aid in both humanitarian and military endeavors related to national security.

- **National Reconnaissance Office (NRO):** Under the Department of Defense, the NRO designs, produces, and runs all US reconnaissance satellites and is staffed by both DOD and CIA personnel.

- **National Security Agency/Central Security Service (NSA):** The NSA gathers and analyzes signals intelligence and works to safeguard American information systems.

- **Air Force Intelligence:** This military agency gathers intelligence from sensors in the air, in space, and even in cyberspace for the US Air Force.

- **Army Intelligence and Security Command (INSCOM):** This military agency oversees all intelligence operations within the US Army.

- **Marine Corps Intelligence:** This military agency provides intelligence for battlefield support of the US Marine Corps.

- **Office of Naval Intelligence (ONI):** This military agency provides maritime intelligence to the Navy, other defense branches working with the Navy, other agencies in the IC, and US policymakers.

Q: Which entity is the largest employer of mathematicians in the United States?

A: Founded in 1952 to handle US signals intelligence and, therefore, cryptography, the NSA is thought to be the largest employer of mathematicians in the United States.

Q: What are the many name changes that Russian or Soviet intelligence agencies have gone through?

A: The Tsarist Russian intelligence agency was called the Okhrana. But the lineage of today's Russian agencies can be more directly linked to the Cheka, started in 1917 with the Bolshevik Revolution. In 1922, the Cheka was rebranded as the GPU (State Political Administration) and kept its leader, Feliks Dzerzhinsky. The agency was quickly renamed the OGPU (United State Political Administration). In 1934, it became the NKVD (People's Commissariat for Internal Affairs), headed by Lavrenti Beria. In March 1946, the NKVD was broken up into the MVD (Ministry of Internal Affairs, still under Beria) and the MGB (Ministry of State Security). In 1954, the KGB was created. In 1991, the KGB was broken up into the FSB (Federal Security Service) and the SVR (Foreign Intelligence Service).

Q: How did the KGB come into being?

A: The KGB is probably the best-known iteration of Russian intelligence, perhaps because it existed from 1954 to 1991, spanning much of the Cold War, and it has been mentioned in a lot of spy books and movies. After Stalin died, many of the remaining leaders of the Communist Party, including future Russian leader Nikita Khrushchev, turned on the head of the MVD, Lavrenti Beria.

They had him tried for false crimes against the state (although he did commit real crimes against humanity), and he was executed in 1953. In 1954, they also reorganized and renamed the agency to the KGB, meaning the Committee for State Security. The organization ran intelligence and counterintelligence operations on the West and spied on its own people. The KGB even had its own training school. See page 186 for details of the fate of the KGB.

Q: Which spy agency's building is nicknamed Legoland?

A: The headquarters for MI6 in London, built in 1994 when the agency was renamed to Her Britannic Majesty's Secret Intelligence Service (SIS), is referred to as Legoland because of its construction, which looks like a bunch of layered pieces stuck together.

Q : What became of the KGB after the fall of the Soviet Union in 1991?

A : In 1991, when the Soviet Union was dismantled, the statue of Feliks Dzerzhinsky, head of the first two post-Bolshevik revolution Russian intelligence services, at KGB headquarters in Moscow was removed. The KGB was reorganized into the intelligence service of the new Russian Federation and broken into two agencies: the FSB, which handles domestic intelligence, and the SVR, which handles external intelligence.

Higher-ups from the former KGB rose to power in Russia, including former KGB and FSB official Vladimir Putin, who was made prime minister in 1999 under President Boris Yeltsin. Then Yeltsin resigned and made Putin acting president. Putin was officially elected president in 2000.

Chechen terrorism fears played a role in his election, after a series of bombings of apartment buildings in 1999. Some thought the Russian government was responsible for the bombings, including former KGB and FSB agent Alexander Litvinenko, who alleged just that in a book. He was mysteriously poisoned with polonium-210 in 2006.

Q: Britain denied the existence of which intelligence service until 1994?

A: The British intelligence agency Military Intelligence Section 6 (or MI6) was created in 1909 due to threats from Germany. But the British government denied its existence until a 1994 act of Parliament that renamed it Her Britannic Majesty's Secret Intelligence Service (SIS). People often still refer to it as MI6.

Q: How do underlings refer to the head of the SIS?

A: Like M in the Bond films, the head of the SIS (or MI6) is also referred to by a letter: C. This practice is an homage to the first head of MI6, Sir Mansfield George Smith-Cumming, who signed documents with his initial, C. The head of SIS still signs documents or correspondence with the letter C, in green ink.

Q: What is the difference between MI5 and MI6?

A: The Security Service (formerly named Military Intelligence Section 5 and often still referred to as MI5) handles and safeguards intelligence internal to the UK, and the SIS (commonly still referred to as MI6) gathers intelligence from outside the UK. MI5 is akin to the United States' FBI, and MI6 is more like the CIA.

Q: What are some of Israeli intelligence agency Mossad's notable exploits?

A: In 1947, the UN passed Resolution 181, which would break Palestine into separate Jewish and Arab states in May 1948. As a result, internal conflict broke out between Jewish and Palestinian groups. When Israel declared independence in May 1948, this conflict grew into war with neighboring states Egypt, Lebanon, Syria, and Jordan (at the time called Transjordan). In 1949, the countries reached agreement on armistice lines and hostilities between the nations ceased for a couple of decades.

On April 1, 1951, Israel created the Institute for Intelligence and Special Operations, more commonly referred to as Mossad (meaning "the institute").

The group reportedly obtained a copy of the 1956 Nikita Khrushchev speech in which he broke with Stalinism.

In May 1960, Mossad and Israel's internal intelligence agency, Shin Bet, captured fugitive Nazi Adolf Eichmann, one of the architects of the Holocaust, in Argentina. They brought him to Jerusalem, where he was put on trial.

When Israel wanted a nuclear weapon to deter invasion, a plan they dubbed the Samson Option, Mossad was tasked with covertly acquiring the necessary uranium ore. The agency worked with a West German company, whose leaders agreed to obtain the ore and lied to the International Atomic Energy Agency, saying it was going to be used for soap manufacturing. Via a front company, they bought a ship in Hamburg, letting the existing crew go but paying them a generous severance.

In November 1968, the new ship's crew transported two hundred tons of uranium ore from Antwerp, Belgium, to no one knows exactly where. As far as international authorities were concerned, the ore was missing. The ship later sailed to Palermo, Sicily, and the crew disembarked and disappeared. Israel doesn't publicly acknowledge its nuclear weapons capability, but it is widely accepted that it has them.

After a Palestinian terrorist group called Black September killed eleven Israeli Olympic athletes during the 1972 Munich Olympics, Mossad set out to get revenge for the killings. Members of the operation, dubbed the Avner group (after one of the members), were purportedly told to resign for plausible deniability on Israel's part. They were tasked with assassinating eleven specific Palestinians around the globe, including Yasser Arafat's cousin. The papers called the mission Wrath of God. The 2005 Steven Spielberg film Munich is about this mission.

Another Mossad team had the mission of assassinating the man thought to have planned the attack, Ali Hassan Salameh. In 1973, they killed a waiter in Lillehammer, Norway, who they thought was Salameh, but he turned out to be an innocent Moroccan man. The team was arrested by Norwegian police. Salameh was killed in 1979 when his car was bombed in Beirut.

In 1976, Mossad intervened in a hostage crisis. Palestinian terrorists hijacked an Air France plane on its layover in Athens, Greece. The terrorist demanded the release of Palestinian and German prisoners in Israel and flew the plane to Entebbe, Uganda. They released the non-Jewish hostages and threatened to blow up the plane. In Operation Thunderbolt, Israeli special forces swooped in and rescued most of the hostages and crew within a few minutes, although four hostages were killed. Future Prime Minister of Israel Benjamin Netanyahu's elder brother was in the special forces team, and he was killed during the rescue mission.

Q: What operation to rescue thousands of refugees involved running a scuba-diving resort for cover?

A: In the late 1970s, Israeli intelligence agency Mossad hatched a plan to exfiltrate thousands of a community known as the Beta Israel (which translates to "House of Israel") out of Ethiopia. The group consisted of tens of thousands of Ethiopian descendants of the Hebrews who had been cut off from other Jewish societies around 2,500 years ago. In the 1970s, many of the Beta Israel, along with other Ethiopians, fled to the UN-run refugee camps at the border of Ethiopia and Sudan. In 1977, Israel ruled that they were eligible for the right of return to Israel, where they would gain automatic Israeli citizenship.

The Beta Israel were already suffering the hardships of all Ethiopians (war, drought, and famine), but there was an extra peril for them: Sudan was hostile to Israel, and being Jewish could be dangerous in the area where the refugee camps were located. The head of Mossad, Efraim Halevy, enlisted Dani Limor to lead an unprecedented mission, named Operation Brothers, to get them out of the country.

In August 1981, Limor went into Sudan undercover as a French-speaking archeologist. While he was driving around, he passed an abandoned hotel near the coast and asked about it. It was the shut-down Arous Hotel, which had been a scuba-diving resort but had no running water and bad road access. So Mossad got into the hotel business, and the team used it as their base.

The operatives didn't just stay at the hotel. They hired a scuba-diving instructor named Rubi Viterbo (who also happened to be an ex Israeli Navy Seal) and one of his students, Yola Reitman, to run the place and act as operatives (the first time Mossad used civilians in a covert mission). To give a further air of legitimacy, they created a hotel brochure and placed magazine ads. They got guests, and at some point, the hotel was making good money.

They were ready to embark on their real mission sometime in the spring of 1982. The plan was to get the Beta Israel refugees out of the camps to the coast of Sudan, where Navy Seals would take them to a ship called the *Bat Galim*, which would be waiting in international waters. They would send out trucks in the night with the cover story that they were on a supply run, go to a spot near the camps, have someone guide groups of the refugees to the trucks, and take off for the coast.

They could only carry around two hundred people at a time, and they had to talk their way through several military roadblocks. Limor said he would take the lead and get the guards talking, offering them cigarettes and biscuits (cookies). When the trucks holding the refugees came by, he'd say they were with him, and they'd get waved through. They'd radio Reitman when they were past the last roadblock, and she would radio the Navy team to let them know. Then they'd make the long trek to the beach, where Navy Seals would take the refugees to the ship in small boats.

It worked four times over six months without a hitch, but on the fifth run on March 10, 1982, Sudanese army soldiers started shooting at the last group of refugees before the Seals got the boat into the water. When Limor ran at them and yelled that they were tourists, the military left them alone, and they were able to leave. But Mossad deemed that it was too dangerous to continue and ordered the team to evacuate the hotel. Limor went back to Israel and talked them out of the evacuation, but they decided to find another rescue method.

Mossad settled on trying to fly people out. The team found a landing spot with the right specifications for a makeshift runway about 120 miles from the refugee camp. In May 1982, two C-130 military planes that could hold around two hundred people each were flown out of Israel at night. They stayed low to avoid radar. Part of the team got the refugees to the site while the others directed the pilots to the landing spot. The pilots used night vision goggles due to the lack of runway lights, and radio communication was in English.

The team managed seventeen air rescues between summer 1982 and fall 1984, extricating approximately twelve thousand Beta Israel refugees and bringing them to Israel. Sometime in 1985, news of missions got out, and Mossad ordered the hotel evacuated again. This time they complied and left in the night. Guests woke up to a staff-less hotel.

US Vice President George H. W. Bush talked with Sudanese President Jaafar an-Nimeiry in secret and negotiated 258 airlifts. Israel and the US ran more missions to carry people over to Israel: Operation Moses, Operation Joshua, and Operation Solomon. Around 130,000 Hebrews of Ethiopian descent lived in Israel as of 2019.

A: In 1985, FBI arrests of several people working in the US intelligence community made the news:

Jonathan Jay Pollard worked as a civilian analyst for the Office of Naval Intelligence (ONI) at the US Navy's Anti-Terrorist Alert Center in Maryland. Coworkers saw him carrying classified documents out of the building. The FBI began monitoring him, and when he did it again, they brought him in for questioning. Pollard and his wife, who was also involved, tried to seek asylum at the Israeli embassy, but they were refused and arrested right outside the embassy. It turned out that Pollard had volunteered to spy for Israel and had sold them more than a million documents, some highly sensitive, including electronic communications procedures, the subsequent changing of which cost the government billions of dollars. His handler had diplomatic cover at the Israeli embassy. Pollard got a life sentence in 1987. Groups of Americans and Israelis made several pushes to get him pardoned by the president, attempts opposed by US intelligence and national security entities. Although the pardon didn't happen, he was paroled in 2015.

John Anthony Walker, Jr., was a warrant officer in the US Navy. Around 1967, he contacted the Soviet Union via their embassy and started passing cryptographic secrets to them, including communication codes. He photographed documents with a Minox camera, and he and his Soviet handlers used 7UP cans to signal readiness for a drop. After he retired in 1976, he created a spy ring by recruiting his best friend Jerry Whitworth, his brother Arthur, and his son Michael (stationed on the USS *Nimitz*), all government workers with security clearance, to spy for the Soviets. He tried unsuccessfully to recruit his wife and daughter (the latter in the Army). After divorcing him, his wife called the FBI. Unfortunately, they didn't believe her. But in 1984, she repeated the charge. The intel Walker handed over to the Soviets was estimated to have compromised around a million classified messages. On May 20, 1985, Walker was arrested after a dead drop of intel in Poolesville, Maryland. He pleaded guilty and received a life sentence.

Sharon Marie Scranage, a CIA clerk in Ghana, was found to have passed the identities of CIA assets and other state secrets to a man she was dating, Michael Soussoudis, cousin to the Ghanaian head of state at the time. The CIA became suspicious after her results on a routine polygraph test. She and Soussoudis were charged in July 1985 and pleaded guilty. She received a five-year sentence.

Larry Wu-tai Chin was a CIA officer and Chinese language translator for nearly thirty years. He was found to have been working for the Chinese government, passing CIA documents and photographs to them. He was arrested on November 22, 1985. He was convicted, but before sentencing, he committed suicide.

Ronald William Pelton was a communications specialist with the National Security Agency (NSA). He quit his job in 1979. Due to money problems, he walked into the Soviet Embassy in Washington, DC, and offered his services. Although he no longer worked at the NSA, he had one thing that compensated for lack of access—a photographic memory. He provided secrets to the Soviets for several years but was found out when a KGB defector told on him. The FBI arrested Pelton on November 25, 1985. He was convicted in 1986 and got three life sentences.

A spy book became very popular in 1985. President Ronald Reagan raved about *The Hunt for Red October* by Tom Clancy at a press conference, saying it was the "perfect yarn." It's about the Lithuanian captain of a secret high-tech Soviet submarine, Marko Ramius, who wants to defect to the US, along with several officers, and hand over the vessel. The book (in the now well-known Jack Ryan series) became a best seller.

There were other spies working in the US at the time who weren't discovered until later, like Aldrich Ames, a CIA counterintelligence agent who spied for the Soviets and post-Soviet Russia for nine years, and Robert P. Hanssen, an FBI agent who did the same for over twenty years.

The title might really belong to 1984, during which even more spies (twelve in all) were arrested by the FBI.

CHAPTER 10

RATFUCKING
POLITICAL HITS AND DIRTY TRICKS

Q: Which president resigned in disgrace over an espionage cover-up scandal?

A: On June 17, 1972, five men broke into the Democratic National Committee (DNC) offices at the Watergate Hotel (which was also an apartment complex and office space). They were caught in the act, and were found with incriminating evidence like bugging equipment. Four of the men (Bernard L. Barker, Virgilio Gonzalez, Eugenio Martinez, and Frank Sturgis) turned out to be operatives who had worked with the CIA in efforts to oust Cuba's leader, Fidel Castro, and the fifth was James McCord, security chief of President Richard Nixon's Committee to Re-elect the President (later dubbed CREEP).

Two reporters at the *Washington Post*, Carl Bernstein and Bob Woodward (among others) continued to dig into the story and uncovered two coconspirators: E. Howard Hunt, Jr., (a former CIA agent turned operative for the president's campaign) and G. Gordon Liddy (a former FBI agent acting as counsel for CREEP). The crew at the *Washington Post* made discovery after discovery (as did some other papers like the *New York Times*), implicating many people in the president's circle and getting closer and closer to the president. The operatives working for the president's campaign were also called the Plumbers because they had initially been set up to stop information leaks.

The administration in the White House insisted that the allegations weren't true and that the *Washington Post* was a liberal paper out to get Nixon. Despite the ongoing scandal, Nixon won the 1972 presidential election against George McGovern in a landslide victory.

When the five burglars and two conspirators were tried, all either pleaded or were found guilty. The Senate then voted unanimously to create the Select Committee on Presidential Campaign Activities to investigate potential abuses in Nixon's reelection campaign. Nixon tried to stop his aides from testifying before the committee, citing executive privilege. Samuel J. Ervin, Jr., the presiding senator, threatened to issue arrest warrants for anyone who refused to testify. A Watergate grand jury was convened and Archibald Cox, Jr., was named special prosecutor.

At the sentencing for the original Watergate burglary trial, McCord gave Judge John J. Sirica a note saying that the group had been pressured to keep quiet and plead guilty by higher-ups and that some of the testimony included perjury. Sirica set the stage for further revelations when he handed down long sentences, but said he'd lower them if they told the truth before the Senate or the grand jury.

All three major networks aired the Senate hearings, initially in their entirety (resulting in preempting of many TV shows), then in their entirety on some PBS stations and in rotation on the commercial networks. Revelations included many acts of wrongdoing by White House staffers, including wiretapping, money laundering, and various acts of sabotage to hurt Democratic candidates (operations the group called "ratfucking").

Other White House operatives eventually found to be involved in the scandal included Charles Colson (special advisor to the president), John Dean (White House counsel), John Ehrlichman (the president's adviser for domestic affairs), H. R. Haldeman (White House chief of staff), Jeb Magruder (White House communications adviser), John Mitchell (first attorney general, then director of CREEP), and Donald Segretti (former military prosecutor turned CREEP operative).

For Woodward and Bernstein's part in the revelations, an informant the reporters called Deep Throat (after a popular 1972 porn film) was feeding Woodward tips and both reporters followed up on them. Woodward and his informant had late-night meetings in an underground parking garage. They would set up the meetings via covert signals. Woodward would move a flowerpot with a red flag sticking out of it when he wanted to meet. Deep Throat would mark page 20 of Woodward's copy of the *New York Times*.

Despite attacks on all fronts, President Nixon maintained his innocence. Nixon's former counsel John Dean testified that Nixon was in charge of the Watergate operation and an effort to cover up his involvement, but there was no other direct evidence. That is, until one of the reporters tipped someone working on the Senate hearings about a witness they should call: Alexander P. Butterfield, former deputy assistant to the president. Butterfield made a revelation that led to the "smoking gun" everyone was looking for—the president had all conversations in his offices secretly recorded.

Ervin and Cox subpoenaed tapes of relevant conversations. Nixon refused, once again invoking executive privilege. Sirica's court and an appeals court ordered them turned over.

Nixon told his attorney general, Elliot Richardson, to fire special prosecutor Cox. Richardson and his deputy attorney general, William D. Ruckelshaus, both resigned rather than carry out the order (a chain of events called the Saturday Night Massacre). Solicitor general Robert Bork fired Cox, who was replaced by Leon Jaworski. After public outcry over the events, Nixon released most of the requested tapes (seven of nine). On one of the tapes, eighteen minutes had been erased. He was ordered to turn over three more tapes, but instead of the tapes handed over transcripts. But even the transcripts showed that Nixon was directly involved in the cover-up.

The House Judiciary Committee started an impeachment inquiry and passed articles of impeachment. Nixon resigned on August 8, 1974. Vice President Gerald Ford, now president, preemptively pardoned Nixon on September 8, 1974.

In 2005, Deep Throat was revealed to have been deputy director of the FBI W. Mark Felt, Sr. (second in command at the FBI during the Watergate scandal). Watergate was so huge that many scandals since have been suffixed with "gate."

Q: What revelations prompted heavy oversight of the CIA and FBI after the Watergate scandal?

A: From 1973 to 1975, several revelations, some from the CIA itself, about illegal or immoral CIA and FBI operations (often at the behest of the president or the National Security Council), prompted public outrage and led to strict congressional oversight of the agencies in the US intelligence community.

Some of the operations under scrutiny were assassination attempts against Fidel Castro (prime minister of Cuba), Patrice Lumumba (prime minister of the Democratic Republic of the Congo), and Salvador Allende (president of Chile), all in the name of stopping the spread of communism, but none successfully carried out. The Castro plans, developed by the CIA's technical support division (TSD), included possibly dusting his beard, spraying his wetsuit with poison, or (in one plan reminiscent of a Looney Tunes cartoon) giving him an exploding cigar. Another plot they considered involved hiring Sam Giancana and John Rosselli, members of the Chicago mob.

Other operations included subsidies for cover organizations like the National Student Association, infiltration of domestic civil rights and antiwar groups, and the reading of US citizens' mail going to Soviet Union and Eastern Bloc countries. One operation by the TSD called Project MK-ULTRA (formerly Operation Bluebird) was a drug-testing program that administered heroin, amphetamines, and LSD to CIA employees without their knowledge to see if they could achieve mind control (the project resulted in the death of Army bioweapons researcher Dr. Frank Olson, who was surreptitiously given LSD and jumped off a building).

From 1975 to 1976, Senator Frank Church led the Select Committee to Study Government Operations with Respect to

Intelligence Activities, or the Church Committee, to investigate the wrongdoing of the CIA, FBI, NSA, and other agencies.

President Gerald Ford and President Jimmy Carter both signed executive orders that put restrictions on the Intelligence Community and banned assassination attempts.

Q: What precipitated eight US embassy officials being expelled from Paris?

A: In December 1994, Charles Pasqua, the French minister of interior, called Pamela Harriman, the US ambassador to France, to his office. He presented her with conversation summaries and photographs of meetings between US diplomats and French officials, alleging that the Americans were inappropriately trying to gather intel about foreign contract negotiations and the state of the country's telecommunications. He insisted the diplomats be expelled from France. Many details about the meeting were widely reported in the French press to a level that is unusual for an event related to spying between allied intelligence agencies.

It is suspected that the information was leaked to draw attention away from a scandal involving Premier Édoaurd Balladur and an alleged bribe to a magistrate while Balladur was up for reelection. Another possible element is a business relationship between Balladur's son and an American attorney, who the Direction de la Surveillance du Territoire, or DST suspected of being connected with US intelligence. The relationship between the two governments soured for a few months but went back to nearly normal after Balladur lost the election.

CHAPTER 11

BIG BROTHER

SPYING WITHIN

Q: What revolutionary group ostensibly against the Bolsheviks was actually a ploy by Russian intelligence to catch would-be dissidents?

A: After the Bolshevik Revolution of 1917 and the Russian Civil War that ensued, a group called The Trust was created with the purported mission of opposing the new Bolshevik government. People joined the group, but the Russian intelligence agency OGPU (the successor to the Cheka, both headed by Feliks Dzerzhinsky) was able to keep tabs on all its members, because the OGPU had set up the group.

The OGPU would follow activities of the group and then jail participating members. They even roped in exiles living outside of Russia, in some cases luring them back to their home country and executing them.

One such Russian exile was Sidney Reilly (real name Shlomo Rosenblum), a womanizer, conman, alleged murderer, and spy for MI6. Riley had been sentenced to death for counterrevolutionary activities against Lenin in 1918 but escaped and was living in exile in Britain. He thought The Trust was a real anti-Bolshevik organization and was enticed into returning to Russia, where he was immediately arrested. Stalin ordered his execution, and Reilly was shot in November 1925.

A: Historians aren't sure of the real circumstances surrounding Sergei Kirov's murder. Some speculate that Stalin himself ordered the assassination. But whatever the case, Stalin claimed Kirov's murder was a sign of an internal conspiracy to get rid of Bolshevik party leaders and used it as an excuse for launching one of the most infamous killing sprees in history: the Great Purge.

He concocted a network of spies who were supposedly plotting against his regime and put forth propaganda encouraging citizens to denounce enemies of the state. People were denouncing their own enemies or rivals. He tasked his newly renamed secret police (now the NKVD) with arresting, torturing, and getting confessions out of scores of innocent people. In all, Stalin's purges from 1936 to 1938 resulted in the execution of at least six hundred thousand people.

After the war, he was paranoid about anyone who had been exposed to the West, even his own soldiers, out of fear that they could be spies. When Russian soldiers returned home from WWII, they were imprisoned in a system of forced labor camps called the Gulag.

In a bit of irony, his purges and other paranoid affronts may have contributed to his death, or at least greatly diminished the medical care he received when he collapsed in 1953. In 1951, a physician advised Stalin to rest, which he did not like, so he had the doctor arrested as a spy for the Brits. And in 1952, Stalin had many Jewish doctors in Moscow arrested, claiming they were plotting to poison him and others at the behest of America. Their trials were pending at the time of his collapse. One doctor on trial even recounted suddenly being asked medical questions while being interrogated. So there was a shortage of doctors, and the ones who were there were visibly nervous. Stalin died on March 5, 1953.

Q: What East German intelligence group spied on just about everyone in the country?

A: East Germany's Ministry for State Security (Stasi) referred to themselves as "The Firm" and as the "Shield and Sword of the Party." Some of its officers were trained by the KGB. The agency spied both abroad and on their own people on a massive scale.

From 1957 to 1989, the Stasi was led by Erich Mielke, a working-class German Communist Party member with a past. He fled to Russia after killing two police officers in a riot in Berlin and serving a short sentence. He returned after WWII when half of Germany was handed over to Russia.

The Stasi also spied on West Germany and got moles into businesses and government.

They sometimes blackmailed people into spying for them. One tactic involved "Romeo operations," like a gender-specific "honey pot" where male agents targeted female secretaries. One secretary in the foreign ministry committed suicide because she found out that her husband had only married her for access to intelligence.

They kept the population in constant fear. East Germany had a population of 16 million with around 91,000 agents and 173,000 informants by 1989. The Stasi couldn't be everywhere, but people didn't know whether they were being monitored or not. Those who tried to leave East Germany without permission were often shot.

The files of their incredibly thorough surveillance on East German citizens are said to have spanned 111 miles. When the Berlin Wall fell in 1989, the Stasi was dissolved, and people were allowed to look into their own files, sometimes to find out that their spouses or other loved ones had informed on them.

The Stasi headquarters and Hohenschönhausen prison (which was used by the Stasi as a center of operations and where many of the organization's victims were interrogated, tortured, and imprisoned) have been turned into museums. The prison tour guides are dissidents who were formerly held in the prison.

The 2006 film *The Lives of Others* is about a Stasi employee listening in on people in East Germany.

Q: What illegal FBI program had the aim of disrupting "subversive" groups of US citizens?

A: COINTELPRO (short for Counterintelligence Program) was an FBI operation that ran from 1956 to 1971 (at the time under the leadership of J. Edgar Hoover). The program's initial aim was to disrupt the Communist Party of the United States, but in the 1960s, it was expanded to include other groups the FBI considered subversive, and its operations were often illegal.

Targets included communist and socialist organizations, anti-war activist groups, civil rights organizations (such as the Black Panther Party, Dr. Martin Luther King, Jr.'s Southern Christian Leadership Conference, and the American Indian Movement), and (more understandably) hate groups (such as the KKK and the American Nazi Party), to name just a few.

The organizations were surveilled, infiltrated, harassed by law enforcement, and disrupted in a variety of ways in an effort to thwart and silence them. In one outrageous operation, anonymous blackmail letters were sent to Dr. King in an effort to make him commit suicide. In another actually deadly one, the FBI gave intel to the Chicago police that helped them raid Black Panther Party leader Fred Hampton's home, resulting in his death at the hands of police.

On March 8, 1971, a group of people calling themselves the Citizens' Commission to Investigate the FBI broke into an FBIs office in Media, Pennsylvania, stole files related to COINTELPRO, and sent them to several congressmen and newspapers. Nixon tried to get the papers to kill the story and return the government documents, and the *Washington Post* (which also broke the Watergate scandal) was the only one to run the story initially.

Miraculously, the group of activist burglars were never caught despite the fact that two hundred FBI agents were assigned to investigate until the statute of limitations expired. The group had done meticulous work casing the office, wore gloves so that they didn't leave fingerprints, and never met with each other after their covert act.

The Church Committee (the United States Senate Select Committee to Study Governmental Operations with Respect to Intelligence Activities, headed by Senator Frank Church) looked into the available information and censured the FBI for an operation that thwarted citizens' First Amendment—granted freedoms of speech and association.

More has since come out from agents involved in the program and through Freedom of Information Act requests. In 2014, four of the eight Citizens' Commission members revealed their identities: Bob Williamson, Keith Forsyth, and John and Bonnie Raines. Another, William C. Davidon, the initiator of the plan, intended to reveal his involvement, as well, but he died from Parkinson's disease in 2013. The other three remain anonymous.

CHAPTER 12

THE WAR ON TERROR

Q : What covert terrorist attack was the most deadly ever perpetrated on US soil?

A : Osama bin Laden, a son of a rich Saudi Arabian family, was a leader in the Mujahideen fighting in Afghanistan during the Russian invasion from 1979 to 1989. After that conflict ended, he formed a terrorist group called Al Qaeda (which means "the Base"). In 1990, he offered to have his group defend Saudi Arabia against Iraq, but the offer was rejected. Saudi Arabia allied with the US in the Persian Gulf War, incensing bin Laden, and he settled in Sudan.

Al Qaeda ambushed and killed American troops in Somalia in 1993. In 1996, Sudan expelled bin Laden and he went back to decimated and now Taliban-run Afghanistan. There, he issued a fatwa (i.e. declared holy war) on the US. Al Qaeda ran training camps in Afghanistan. In 1998, the group bombed US embassies in Africa in Dar es Salaam, Kenya, Nairobi, and Tanzania simultaneously, killing over two hundred people. In 2000, Al Qaeda bombed the warship USS *Cole* in the waters off Yemen. But the worst was yet to come.

On September 11, 2001, nineteen of bin Laden's terrorist trainees hijacked four passenger planes and flew two of them into the Twin Towers in New York (causing the buildings to collapse) and one into the Pentagon in Washington, DC. They attempted to strike another target (possibly the White House) with the fourth, but that one was foiled by brave passengers who stopped them from reaching the target (sadly the plane crashed in Pennsylvania, killing all on board). Nearly three thousand in all were killed in the attacks, including hundreds of emergency responders. This was a disaster both in terms of the toll in human life and in the lack of detection by US intelligence.

The attack led to President George W. Bush declaring a war on terror, to US and British forces invading Afghanistan in October 2001, and to the signing of the Uniting and Strengthening America by Providing Appropriate Tools Required to Intercept and Obstruct Terrorism Act of 2001 (aka the USA PATRIOT Act), which expanded the surveillance authority of US intelligence and law enforcement agencies.

During this new Afghan war, the Taliban were ousted from power and Al Qaeda lost its base in Afghanistan, but bin Laden escaped and continued activities, and the war raged on.

In 2002, President Bush and the US Congress formed the National Commission on Terrorist Attacks Upon the United States (aka the 9/11 Commission) to investigate where US intelligence had failed. They found that the various US intelligence agencies weren't sharing data effectively and that none of them had ever imagined that scenario.

In 2003, the US government used the war on terror and faulty intel on supposed weapons of mass destruction (WMDs) in Iraq as an excuse to invade Iraq and oust its leader, Saddam Hussein. Ultimately, no WMDs were found.

In 2004, the US established a new director of National Intelligence position to oversee all US intelligence agencies at the suggestion of the 9/11 Commission. In 2005, the Office of the Director of Central Intelligence (at the CIA) was eliminated.

The US continued to search for bin Laden. In summer 2010, the CIA traced a man thought to be a courier for bin Laden to a compound in Abbottabad, Pakistan (an urban area named for Sir James Abbott, a former British administrator in India and Pakistan). Agents were stationed in a nearby house to monitor the residence, and spy satellites were trained on the compound. They couldn't tap into the compound's phone or internet activities because it didn't have them. The residence was off the grid, so to speak.

A mission to catch bin Laden was hatched by the Joint Special Operations Command and the CIA. A mockup of his compound was built and a potential raid was rehearsed. President Barack Obama ordered the raid. On May 2, 2011, they flew in helicopters and attacked the compound, and after forty minutes of gunfire, bin Laden was dead.

Q : What sugary powdered drink played a role in a large terrorist plot uncovered by MI5?

A : Tang made an appearance in an Al Qaeda plot to blow up airliners flying from Britain to the US and Canada. A cell in England planned to use the powdered drink as an accelerant in homemade liquid explosive devices made with plastic soda bottles, hydrogen peroxide, and hexamethylene triperoxide diamine hidden in the shells of AA batteries.

Fortunately, MI5 was onto the terrorists. During spring or early summer 2006, they got wind that Abdulla Ahmed Ali, already suspected of having terrorist ties, was planning some sort of attack. On June 24, 2006, Ali returned on a flight from Pakistan to London. Agents secretly searched his bags at Heathrow Airport.

As part of Operation OVERT, MI5 and Scotland Yard started constant surveillance of Ali (the ringleader) and his associates. In late July, Ali moved into an apartment owned by his brother. MI5 broke in and installed recording devices. British intelligence collected gobs of information, including audio recordings, video footage, and in-person agent surveillance. The CIA, NSA, and other US intelligence agencies also assisted in intel gathering.

In some of the audio recordings, terrorists were overheard saying something that indicated they planned to have nineteen bombers, just as in the 9/11 attack. They even toyed with the idea of bringing their own families as cover. The group also recorded suicide videos.

Some members of the cell applied for new passports. Ali was monitored researching flight timetables between August and October.

The Brits wanted to hold off and gather more evidence, but the CIA pushed Pakistani authorities to arrest one of the conspirators, Rashid Rauf, immediately. On August 9, 2006, Pakistan arrested Rauf. Shortly thereafter, MI5 and the Metropolitan Police rushed to arrest the rest of the plotters, including Ali, before they could act. There were twenty-four arrests in all.

The investigation was largest surveillance operation to date in the United Kingdom. This incident led to airports banning liquids on flights to prevent the possibility of a similar plot.

Q: What CIA and MI6 plots led to the ouster of an Iranian Prime Minister?

A: In 1953, Prime Minister Mohammad Mosaddegh of Iran announced that Iran was going to nationalize the oil industry. Both American and British intelligence, which had interests in the oil industry there, mobilized to oust Mosaddegh by starting riots and encouraging revolt: the CIA with Operation Ajax and MI6 with Operation Boot. Mosaddegh was arrested and exiled.

Q: Which former Russian spy is known as the "Merchant of Death"?

A: On March 10, 1985, Mikhail Gorbachev became general secretary of the Communist Party of the Soviet Union (CPSU), and in 1988 was elected chairman of the Presidium of the Supreme Soviet (a post that made him de facto president of the USSR). He undertook reforms dubbed perestroika and glasnost, the former to restructure and democratize the government and the latter to soften totalitarian rule and allow more freedom of expression. He also sought better relations with the West, entered into agreements to reduce the nuclear stockpile, removed troops from Afghanistan, and began withdrawing troops from Eastern Bloc countries.

He had a new legislative body created (the USSR Congress of People's Deputies) that was elected by the people. That body appointed a new Supreme Soviet and made Gorbachev its chairman. In 1990, the Congress of the People's Deputies created the post president of the USSR and appointed Gorbachev.

The CPSU was weakened considerably by these reforms and the hardcore party members were not happy. In 1991, a group of them dubbed the Gang of Eight attempted a coup against Gorbachev. President of Russia Boris Yeltsin, other reformers, and protestors resisted the coup. It was foiled and its fomenters were arrested. Gorbachev allied with Yeltsin and began the work of dismantling the Soviet Union and shifting control to the Russian government.

The chaos that ensued set the stage for a new sort of entrepreneur like Viktor Bout. Bout was a Russian military intelligence operative stationed in Africa. He had attended the Soviet Union's Military Institute of Foreign Languages and could speak a bunch of tongues, including several African languages. The dissolution of the USSR left him out of a job. But he still had Kremlin connections, and either bought or was given Soviet military cargo planes, which he used to start a freight company in the UAE importing Western goods into Russia.

Then he decided to go into an even more lucrative business: gun running. He sold Kalashnikovs, tanks, land mines, and other arms and ammo to governments and groups in war-torn areas in Africa. He'd sell to both sides of a conflict in some cases, contributing to massive loss of life.

Bout also sold arms in Afghanistan during the incursion of the Taliban. His initial deals were with the Afghan government, but the Taliban forced a meeting with him by forcing a cargo plane carrying 3 million rounds of AK-47 ammo down, taking the ammo, and kidnapping the crew. He met with Taliban leader Mullah Mohammed Omar and struck a deal to supply arms to the Taliban.

He drew the attention of British minister of state for the Foreign and Commonwealth Office, Peter Hain. In November 2000, Hain used his parliamentary privilege to make a speech mentioning Bout and calling him a merchant of death. The speech and the Merchant of Death headlines that followed drew the attention of intelligence agencies.

In 2002, Interpol put out a red notice (a sort of global arrest warrant) on Bout for weapons trafficking and money laundering. After this, Bout confined himself to Russia under the protection of the government, now run by Vladimir Putin.

The US suffered an embarrassment when someone realized that one of the freight companies used by the US military was connected to Bout, and that the Pentagon had paid them around $60 million.

In 2007, the United States Drug Enforcement Agency (DEA) put together an international operation to take down Bout, dubbed Operation Relentless. They used a real guerrilla group in Colombia, called the FARC to concoct a fake arms deal and set about trying to contact Bout.

They were able to track down someone who had worked with him in South Africa, Andrew Smulian, and convince him to contact Bout about a new deal. He set up a meeting with an undercover DEA agent code-named Carlos, who was a former intelligence operative and drug trafficker in Guatemala.

Carlos and Smulian met in Curacao in January 2008. Smulian called Bout and set up a meeting between Carlos and Bout in Romania, which the DEA had chosen because of their fast extradition process. But that meeting fell through when, due to the Interpol warrant, Bout couldn't get a visa to enter Romania.

They rescheduled the meeting for March at a hotel in Bangkok, Thailand. The DEA worked with Thai police on the operation. Carlos and Bout met in a conference room while agents listened in via a wire on Carlos. The goal was to get him to say aloud that he was selling arms to use against US citizens and to mention what arms he was selling. They really wanted to get him to say he would sell them surface-to-air missiles, because that particular weapon gets an automatic sentence of twenty-five years in prison. And Bout delivered. He said he was an enemy of the US, and offered $15 to 20 million in weapons, including C-4 explosives, grenades, guns, and the missiles. Agents stormed into the room, and Bout was arrested by Thai police.

The US then fought to get Bout extradited, a process lasting over two years due to interference from the Kremlin. He was extradited on November 15, 2010, and in October 2011, he was convicted of four counts of terrorism and sentenced to twenty-five years in a US penitentiary in Illinois. Smulian testified against Bout and got a five-year sentence with time served (making the sentence amount to one more year in jail), and his plea agreement included the possibility of entering the witness protection program.

Q: What plot by the KKK to blow up a Texas energy plant was foiled by the FBI?

A: In the late 1990s, members of a Texas hate group called the True Knights of the Ku Klux Klan had a plan to blow up a natural gas processing plant in Bridgeport, Texas. They were going to place explosives near storage tanks and set them off in hopes of creating a cloud of "sour gas" (hydrogen sulfide) that might kill hundreds, including kids at a nearby school (although a spokesman for the gas company said they only produced nonlethal "sweet gas"). The group also planned to detonate a second explosive when first responders arrived.

But the point of the act wasn't just to sow terror. In a scheme reminiscent of the plot of *Die Hard*, the explosions and possible loss of life were to be distractions they could use to steal $2 million from an armored car, money they intended to use to start a war with the government. The group went about casing the plant and experimenting with improvised explosive devices (IEDs).

Thankfully, the FBI was monitoring the KKK due to their history of acts of terror. They had a mole in the True Knights sect, a member of the group who volunteered because they wanted to prevent the violent act. In what was dubbed "Operation Sour Gas," they surveilled and bugged the known conspirators, and in April 1997 they arrested four members of the group: Catherine Dee Adams, Shawn Dee Adams, Edward Taylor, Jr., and Carl J. Waskom, Jr.

CHAPTER 13

IT'S JUST BUSINESS

INDUSTRIAL ESPIONAGE

Q: Who passed the secrets of Chinese porcelain making to Europe?

A: French-born François Xavier d'Entrecolles became a Jesuit priest in 1682. He was a translator and learned to speak a Chinese language and in 1698, he was sent to do mission work in China. But holy work wasn't his only mission. D'Entrecolles had instructions to find out how the city of Jingdezhen made its white hard-paste porcelain, which was a highly sought-after and very expensive export to Europe at the time.

Over a period of years, he visited porcelain factories, talked with porcelain workers who were converts to Christianity, and read books on the subject. In 1712, he sent correspondence to his superiors explaining the materials and production methods. They wrote back asking for more information, and around ten years later, he sent back more porcelain intel and samples.

But the information came a little late. France was beaten in the European hard-paste porcelain race by Germany, when Johann Friederich Böttger of Dresden developed a method for making it, and his patron, Augustus the Strong, opened a factory producing the stuff. However, several porcelain containers, arguably of the hard-paste variety, were discovered, reportedly made for the second Duke of Buckingham, who died in 1687. This puts in dispute Böttger's status as the first in Europe.

Q: What act of espionage made India the largest producer of tea?

A: The British Empire used to get all their tea from China, the largest tea producer in the world in the 1800s. In fact, Britain traded opium for tea, which incensed the Chinese emperor, who confiscated and destroyed all opium at one point.

In 1843, Robert Fortune, a Scottish self-trained botanist, traveled to China in disguise as a Chinese merchant (because foreigners were not allowed in the interior of the country) collecting plants for the Royal Horticultural Society. He wrote a memoir about the two- to three-year trip. He also learned on that trip that black and green tea come from the same plant and that the difference was in the processing.

In 1848, the East India Trading Company enlisted Fortune to take another trip to China and bring back tea plant seeds and the secrets to cultivating them and producing the final product. He traveled with a servant who was able to ask questions for him, and they talked their way into tours of tea factories.

He discovered their methods and also found out that Chinese manufacturers were using potentially toxic dyes to make the tea going to foreign countries greener because they got more money for that. Fortune brought home the seeds and the secrets, and Britain started cultivating tea in India, which ultimately became the world's largest producer of tea.

Q: Which South American city lost its livelihood to industrial espionage?

A: The city of Manaus, Brazil, lies in the Amazon rainforest north of the Amazon River. In the late nineteenth and early twentieth centuries, the city experienced an economic boom due to demand for rubber—rubber trees were native to the area. The town grew so rich that they installed electric street lights (earlier than most cities in the world), added streetcars, and constructed a lavish opera house called the Teatro Amazonas (the Amazon Theater) that still stands today.

But industrial espionage played a huge role in their economic bust in the 1920s. An English trader smuggled seeds out of the country in 1876, which the British used to cultivate rubber on plantations in British-held areas in Africa and Asia. Once these plantations started producing rubber, they killed Brazil's virtual monopoly, and with it, Manaus's opulent growth. The city is now a major port and is once again prosperous.

Q: What terrible act by the US government was fueled in part by agribusiness wanting to get rid of the competition?

A: The internment of Japanese Americans during World War II was a terrible injustice committed by the US government. It was fueled in part by paranoia that Japanese Americans might spy for Japan after the surprise attack on Pearl Harbor.

Another motivation involved Japanese American farms, which were by and large far more productive than farms run by non-Japanese farmers due to more efficient farming practices. Up to the point of the war, Japanese American farms were producing 40 percent of the produce in California and were worth far more than farms that were run in the traditional American fashion.

Just after the attack on Pearl Harbor, Austin E. Anson, managing secretary of the Salinas Valley Vegetable Grower-Shipper Association, went to Washington, DC, and lobbied for the relocation of Japanese Americans from the West Coast. Other agribusiness entities joined him in the call for exile.

On February 19, 1942, President Roosevelt signed Executive Order 9066 to relocate Japanese Americans away from any area deemed of military importance, and Japanese Americans were shunted off their land in California, Washington, and Oregon. Around 117,000 people of Japanese ancestry were rounded up and relocated. Many were imprisoned in one of ten camps, where living conditions were substandard. Some were shot trying to escape or for getting too near the edges of the camps.

The farms of Japanese Americans were put under government control and doled out to non-Japanese farmers along with loans to help keep them going. Although they weren't the only voices calling for this drastic and inhumane measure, the farm industry enriched itself at the expense of the victims of internment.

The Supreme Court case Endo v. the United States ended internment in 1945, although the last camp wasn't closed until March 1946. In 1988, the government awarded $20,000 per survivor in reparations, totaling around $1.2 billion.

Q: Which Russian agent brought France into the global espionage game?

A: During the period of détente (a lessening of diplomatic tensions) between the US and Russia starting in the late 1960s, the behind-the-scenes spy game continued. The KGB had a department called Directorate T, whose mission was to steal Western technology, military and otherwise—in other words, industrial espionage. Their ring of agents was referred to as Line X, a group started in the 1930s when Russia was stealing technology from Germany. Agents were sent abroad for five years each to gather intel that the Soviet Union could use to advance its own technology and economy, areas in which it was lagging behind the US and others.

The agents gathered intel via open sources at public agencies, connections with major universities like MIT and Caltech, and bribes to people working at tech companies in the US, Europe, and Japan. Then Russian scientists and engineers copied the technology, in some cases beating their Western counterparts to completion.

Vladimir Vetrov (an automobile engineer and KGB agent) was a member of Line X stationed in Paris. His mission was to get to know French scientists and gather intel from them. Vetrov and his wife, Svetlana, enjoyed Paris and openly criticized the Russian system. French intelligence (the DST) was monitoring them and sent an agent named Jacques Prévost to befriend Vetrov and keep tabs on him. In 1970, Vetrov drank too much and got into a car wreck in his embassy-assigned car. He was afraid to tell Russia for fear that he would be sent home. He contacted Prévost, who had the car fixed for him, and Petrov remained in Paris until his five-year stint was up.

Back in Moscow, he and his wife became estranged, and both had affairs. He reportedly felt that the KGB was no longer advancing agents for their abilities and achievements but appointing higher-ups from the nomenklatura (people in the infrastructure of the Communist Party), including Vetrov's boss, and he became disgruntled.

All the technological intel acquired by Line X agents and other methods came through Vetrov's office, and in 1980, he contacted his friend Prévost and offered his services. Prévost contacted Raymond Nart, head of the Soviet division of the French intelligence agency DST.

The DST was small at the time and didn't have any agents abroad. Because they were considered insignificant, Russia had not placed any moles in the agency. The DST tapped Xavier Ameil, a French engineer living in Moscow who had never done any spy work, to handle Vetrov. The two would meet in Vetrov's car, and Vetrov would hand over stacks and binders of documents to Ameil in a plastic bag to be copied and returned a couple of days later. The operation's code name was Farewell. Surprisingly, Vetrov wanted to stay in Russia and keep passing intel to the French rather than return to Paris.

French intelligence soon pulled Ameil out because he was a civilian with no diplomatic immunity and could face death if caught. They switched Vetrov's handler to someone code-named Paul, a military attaché in the French embassy (his identity isn't public knowledge). Vetrov wanted to pass the next batch of documents to a woman at a market, this time on microfilm. Paul sent his wife, and Vetrov used the brush pass method to place the microfilm in her shopping bag. After that, she got cold feet, and Vetrov had to meet with Paul instead, once again in Vetrov's car.

In less than a year, Vetrov passed France around four thousand documents, dubbed the Farewell Dossier, the most intel anyone had gotten out of the Soviet Union to date. It included far more than the West expected Russia to have, including details of all sorts of military and civilian technology, plus all the radio codes of the United States. Vetrov also gave up around 250 Line X agents working abroad.

US intelligence became involved just after France's President, François Mitterrand, visited the US and let President Reagan know about Operation Farewell. The intel gathered by the CIA from the DST and Vetrov was filed under code name Kudo and was classified at a high level of secrecy so that only a few people had access. French and American intelligence started using Vetrov to pass misinformation on Western tech back to Russia, using him as a sort of Trojan horse within the KGB's Directorate T to thwart the Soviet Union's efforts at rapid advancement.

Vetrov began to fall apart mentally. He hooked up with a KGB translator named Ludmilla, who became his mistress. At his final meeting with Paul, Paul said Vetrov smelled of alcohol and repeated, "It's screwed." Vetrov didn't show up for the next meeting, because on February 22, 1982, he and his mistress got into an argument in his parked car and he stabbed her around twenty times. She escaped when someone knocked on the window and distracted Vetrov, and Vetrov stabbed and killed the man. Vetrov reportedly fled the scene but was apprehended when he returned. He was charged with murder and got fifteen years in a prison labor camp in Irkutsk. It was never made clear why he stabbed Ludmilla, but in a letter to his wife, Svetlana, rather than express remorse, he said he regretted not killing her.

His prison cellmate was Valery Rechensky, a KGB counterintelligence officer. From things Vetrov told him, Rechensky thought maybe Vetrov was a double agent. In April 1983, France expelled forty-seven diplomats from the Soviet embassy, making it clear that Russia had a mole. Vetrov was transferred to Lefortovo Prison, a KGB prison in Moscow, and interrogated. He wrote out "The Confessions of a Traitor," a screed condemning everything he thought was wrong with the KGB. Vetrov was executed.

The bad intel he fed to the KGB reportedly resulted in Russia developing and installing faulty technology in a number of areas. Some malicious software passed to Russia via the operation was responsible for a huge Siberian gas pipeline explosion in 1982 that was visible from space, but miraculously didn't kill anyone. Some credit Vladimir Vetrov with speeding up the fall of the USSR.

Q: Which law made it illegal to steal trade secrets from a company?

A: The Economic Espionage Act of 1996 made it illegal to steal, pass, or receive trade secrets with the intent to benefit a foreign power or foreign government–sponsored entity or agent, with penalties up to $500,000 in fines and fifteen years in prison. It also made it illegal to steal, pass, or receive trade secrets for the economic benefit of anyone who is not the owner of the intellectual property, with a penalty of up to ten years in prison and a possible fine. An individual might also face forfeiture of any property obtained by or used in the act of the crime.

A company can be fined up to $10,000,000 for economic espionage and $5,000,000 for theft of trade secrets. The Act defines a trade secret as tangible or intangible financial, business, economic, scientific, or technical information that the owner has taken reasonable measures to keep secret and that derives economic value from not being publicly available.

Q: Which was the first federal case that brought charges under the Economic Espionage Act of 1996?

A: The first case prosecuted under the Economic Espionage Act of 1996 was that of Walter Lian-Heen Liew (aka Liu Yuanxuan). He was indicted in August 2011 and convicted on March 6, 2014 for conspiring to commit economic espionage and steal trade secrets from DuPont in relation to their production of chloride-route titanium dioxide ($TiO2$), an industrial white pigment, and getting them to the People's Republic of China via his California-based company USA Performance Technology, Inc.

Liew apparently gathered former DuPont employees, including Robert Maegerle, to get the technology's secrets and transfer them to Pangang Group companies in China for around $28 million in contracts. The proceeds were put in bank accounts under the names of relatives of Liew's wife, Christina. Liew was also charged with filing false tax returns for USA PTI and another former company, and for bankruptcy fraud, among other related charges.

Liew received the maximum sentence of fifteen years in prison, and was also ordered to forfeit the money made on the contracts and to pay over $500,000 to DuPont and victims of a fraudulent bankruptcy filing. The judge stated that the sentence was intended to send a message that transferring state secrets to a foreign government is a serious crime and threat to US security.

A: Aerospace giant Boeing was in possession of documents belonging to their competitor Lockheed Martin while the two companies were competing for contracts with the US Air Force in the late 1990s. Boeing underbid Lockheed, and the majority of the contracts were awarded to Boeing for their Delta IV rocket, with a few going to Lockheed for their Atlas V rocket. In 1999, Boeing voluntarily divulged to the Air Force and to Lockheed that they had found seven pages of proprietary Lockheed documents in a fired employee's files. But that turned out to be the tip of the iceberg.

In 1997, at a time when Boeing and McDonnell Douglas were merging, then McDonald Douglas employee Bill Erskine (a supervisor on the Delta IV rocket team) hired an engineer from Lockheed named Ken Branch. In 1999, Erskine told a fellow employee, Steve Griffin, that when he'd interviewed Branch, Branch had offered him proprietary Lockheed documents. Griffin, who happened to be married to a Lockheed employee, contacted Boeing's legal department, and Boeing launched an internal investigation. The investigator found Lockheed documents, and Branch and Erskine were both fired. Boeing divulged and turned over the seven pages, and a little later turned over 197 more pages.

Brach filed a wrongful termination lawsuit against Boeing, and Boeing's lawyers made a filing on that case that stated the initial investigation had uncovered a whole box of documents. Boeing then turned over 2,700 additional pages.

In 2003, the Air Force asked Boeing to turn over all Lockheed documents found in Erskine and Branch's files, and a Boeing lawyer sent them around 22,000 pages. After this revelation, the

Air Force reassigned $1 billion in satellite launch contracts from Boeing to Lockheed and banned Boeing from bidding for any more satellite contracts with them.

Boeing claimed that some of the documents weren't handed over earlier because they weren't deemed proprietary, and that others had been misplaced. Later internal reviews revealed the total to be closer to 66,000 pages of Lockheed documents, some in the possession of employees besides the two who were fired.

Lockheed filed a civil suit against Boeing claiming a pattern of economic espionage. One revelation of the suit was that Branch was flown from Florida to Boeing's Huntington Beach, California, office forty-three times during the eighteen-month Air Force contract bidding. Erskine speculated that he was being asked to provide information on Lockheed's Atlas V.

In December 2003, it was discovered that a former Air Force officer, Darleen Druyun, had awarded $5 billion in contracts with the Air Force to Boeing in exchange for jobs for herself and family members, and that she had handed over pricing information from at least one other bidder, maybe more. She was hired by Boeing and fired less than a year after.

In a 2006 plea deal, Branch pleaded guilty to obstruction of justice for getting rid of his laptop during the investigation. The charges of conspiring to steal trade secrets were dropped. He was sentenced to six months' house arrest and a $6,000 fine. Druyun was sentenced to nine months, and Michael Sears, the former CFO who hired her, got four months.

Boeing settled out of court, agreeing to pay $565 million in civil damages and a $50 million fine for criminal charges, without admitting it did anything wrong. Boeing's Delta rocket program was merged with Lockheed's Atlas program.

Q: What was the first foreign economic espionage prosecution in Massachusetts?

A: On June 22, 2006, Elliot Doxer, an employee in finance at Akamai Technologies, Inc., emailed the Israeli consulate in Boston offering them trade secrets, purportedly to help Israel but also asking for money. Someone contacted him in September 2007 and set up a dead drop system where Doxer would leave secrets and pick up instructions in a prearranged place. By March 2009, Doxer had visited the drop site sixty-two times. He disclosed information about the company's employees, customers, accounts, building security system, and computer security.

Unfortunately for Mr. Doxer, the person he was communicating with wasn't an Israeli consulate official, but an undercover agent of the FBI. The government of Israel had cooperated from the beginning. The whole eighteen-month-long operation had been a ruse to gather evidence against him. Doxer was sentenced to six months in jail, six months' house arrest, and a $25,000 fine. It was the eighth such case in the nation and the first in Massachusetts.

Q: Which engineer divulged information about the US space shuttle program to the Chinese government?

A: Dongfan Chung (aka Greg Chung) was born in China but his family emigrated to Taiwan during the Maoist revolutionary fighting in mainland China. He studied engineering in Taiwan, and in 1962, he and his wife, Ling, moved to the US, where Chung attended the University of Minnesota, working on a master's degree. Just after grad school, he got a job at Boeing in Philadelphia. He and his wife became naturalized US citizens.

In 1972, he took a job at Rockwell International, which had just started developing space shuttles for NASA. Chung worked on the shuttle stress-analysis team. Rockwell was acquired by Boeing in 1996, and Chung was once again working for Boeing, from which he retired in 2002. After the tragic breakup of the space shuttle *Columbia* on reentry in 2003, his former boss brought him back to do contract work for the shuttle redesign, and he remained until 2006.

But according to the FBI, he wasn't just doing engineering work during his career of thirty-plus years. He apparently volunteered to send documents on the space shuttle and Delta IV rocket to the People's Republic of China. Although the documents he was caught sharing were unclassified, he reportedly whited out notices that said not to share them outside the company. The document sharing may have gone unnoticed had it not been for an investigation into an operative named Chi Mak, who authorities believed had been purposefully embedded by China in a US company to steal secrets.

Chi Mak, also a California resident, was hired in 1988 at a company called Power Paragon that made power systems for the US Navy. The FBI reportedly received a tip and put Mak under surveillance, including having his phones tapped and regularly digging through his trash. When he and his wife, Rebecca, went on vacation, the FBI searched his house.

Mak was apparently stealing secrets related to Naval ships, submarines, and other technologies, and sending them to China via his brother, Tai Mak, and sister-in-law, Fuk Li. After over a year of surveillance, they overheard Tai and Fuk talking about bringing documents for Chi on a trip to China, and a conversation that seemed to be in code between Tai and someone in China. The FBI arrested them at the airport, and arrested Chi and his wife at their home.

Chi Mak was convicted of conspiring to export military technology and acting as an unregistered agent for China. His wife, Rebecca, pleaded guilty to being an unregistered agent, and Tai, Fuk, and their son Billy pleaded guilty to conspiring with Chi. Chi Mak got twenty-four and a half years in a minimum-security prison. Tai got ten years. Rebecca got three years, after which she was deported, and Fuk and Billy were deported.

During the first search of Mak's house, the FBI found Chung's name in Mak's address book. The FBI asked Chung about Mak, and he said they had dinner occasionally but didn't talk about work. But during a subsequent search, they found a letter addressed to Chung and his wife (in Mak's house) from a Chinese aviation ministry official asking Chung to collect information that would help with China's space program.

The FBI opened an investigation into Chung. They searched his trash and recycling and found Boeing documents. They interviewed him again, and he consented to a search of his house, where they found thousands upon thousands of documents from his job, some on military aircraft, in his basement.

In an interview in 2007, Chi Mak maintained his innocence, saying he hadn't provided any sensitive information, and also saying that Chung wasn't a spy.

In 2009, Chung became the first American convicted by a jury for economic espionage (under the Economic Espionage Act of 1996), and he received a sentence of 188 months (nearly sixteen years) in a minimum-security federal prison. The judge, the same one who had sentenced Chi Mak, said part of the reason for the long sentence was to send a message to China to stop sending spies to the US.

CHAPTER 14

SPIES IN ENTERTAINMENT AND ENTERTAINING SPIES

Q: Which two doomed characters in Shakespeare's play *Hamlet* were enlisted to spy on Hamlet by his mother and stepfather/uncle?

A: Rosencrantz and Guildenstern are ill-fated characters in Shakespeare's famous play *Hamlet*. They are asked to spy on Hamlet, their childhood friend, by his mother, Queen Gertrude, and her husband (and Hamlet's uncle), King Claudius (who Hamlet knows to have killed his father, because his father's ghost told him so).

Hamlet can tell his former friends are being calculating, and he gives them an opportunity to come clean. But they don't. Claudius sends them to escort Hamlet on a ship to England, and Hamlet finds that they have a note instructing the receiver to kill Hamlet. He writes a new note instead saying to kill Rosencrantz and Guildenstern. He then makes his way back home and leaves them to die at the end of their journey.

They are also the titular characters in Tom Stoppard's more comedic play *Rosencrantz and Guildenstern Are Dead*.

Q: What playwright known for writing the basis for two famous operas was also a spy?

A: Pierre-Augustin Caron de Beaumarchais was a Parisian playwright born in 1732. He is famous for writing the plays on which the operas *The Barber of Seville* and *The Marriage of Figaro* were based.

But he had other talents. His father was a watchmaker, and Beaumarchais invented an escapement mechanism (a type of watch mechanism, not anything to do with escaping). He also did covert work for Louis XV and Louis XVI, traveling to England and Germany on covert missions, including to convince the Chevalier d'Éon to return to France (covered on page 65).

He very nearly lost his head in the French Revolution, but a mistress intervened on his behalf.

Q: From which early spy novel did one of the Cambridge Five adopt his name?

A: The novel *Kim* by Rudyard Kipling was an early spy novel published in 1901. The title character is an Irish orphan living in India who can pass as a native. Through odd jobs and by attaching himself to a lama, he begins to learn what is called "the great game" (spy work) and eventually goes on adventures as a spy.

Kim Philby, who was born Harold Philby, adopted a new first name from this novel about his chosen profession.

Q: Which novel by Joseph Conrad was based on a mysterious bombing in England?

A: *The Secret Agent* by Joseph Conrad, published in 1907, revolves around an anti-hero, Verloc, a spy who hangs out with anarchists to foment acts of anarchy for a foreign power that wants the authorities to crack down on revolutionaries. A new embassy chief wants him to blow up the Greenwich Observatory as an act of provocation. Verloc enlists his brother-in-law, Stevie, who has an intellectual disability, to carry out the plot. Before Stevie gets to the building, he stumbles and the bomb explodes, mortally wounding him. Stevie's sister, Verloc's wife, Winnie, stabs Verloc in retaliation when she finds out.

Most of the book is fictitious, but the explosion near the Royal Observatory at Greenwich really happened on February 15, 1894, and it was attributed to anarchists. When the chemical bomb detonated, it blew a hole in the abdomen of the man who was holding it. It also blew off his left hand. The bomber was in possession of a large sum of money. Identified as Martial Bourdin, a 26-year-old Frenchman, he remained conscious for a while, but died in the hospital.

Bourdin was reported to be a member of an anarchist group called Club Autonomie. But no one knows who sent him or if he was a rogue terrorist, or even if he was really headed for the observatory or some other target. David Rooney, curator of the Greenwich Observatory (now a museum), suggested that Bourdin might have intended to blow up the Greenwich Mean Time clock at the gate to the observatory, and not the building itself, since the explosive wasn't powerful enough to do much damage.

Bourdin didn't reveal his intentions before he died, so the true story behind the Greenwich Park explosion remains a mystery.

A: Ian Fleming's first James Bond (007) book, *Casino Royale*, was published in 1953, kicking off one of the most famous spy character franchises of all time. Fleming said Bond wasn't modeled after him, but a composite of the commandos and agents he knew in WWII.

Fleming actually knew two people named James Bond. One was the author of an ornithology book that Fleming liked, and another was a James Charles Bond, who worked as a spy under Fleming during WWII.

A spy with Bond characteristics, if not the name, was Serbian-born Dusko Popov, a suave womanizer with expensive tastes, who played baccarat. Popov was reportedly hired by the Abwehr to spy for Germany in England, but instead, he went immediately to MI6 and became a double agent for Britain (and even, at some point, the Americans). He and Ian Fleming apparently met at the Casino Estoril in Portugal in 1941. Popov even claimed in his autobiography that he was the inspiration for James Bond, and that Casino Royale was based on the Casino Estoril. But Fleming was not alive to confirm or deny his story.

Another oft-mentioned contender is Sidney Reilly, an adventurous Russian-born agent sometimes called the Ace of Spies. Reilly had a knack for languages and, possibly, murder (he allegedly murdered a man to marry his wife and steal his money). He was arrested by the Okhrana, traveled to South America, and settled in Britain, where he adopted his name. He worked for British intelligence, who sent him to China, Persia, Germany, and his original home of Russia on missions. He was a counterrevolutionary with a death sentence on his head in Russia. Unfortunately, he fell for the OGPU's front organization, The Trust, which posed as an anti-

Bolshevik organization to entrap people trying to overthrow the Soviet government. The group enticed him back to Russia, where he was arrested and put to death by order of Stalin. Once again, whether any of his wild exploits influenced Fleming, we'll never know for sure.

Q: Who is the only character featured in all 161 episodes of *The Avengers*?

A: Gentlemanly, bowler-hat wearing, umbrella-carrying secret agent John Steed (Patrick Macnee) was in every single episode of the quirky British spy show *The Avengers*, which ran from 1961 to 1969. Steed had a series of fellow agent partners, starting with Dr. David Keel (Ian Hendry) in season one and Cathy Gale (Honor Blackman) in seasons two and three. His longest-running and arguably most popular partner was Emma Peel (Diana Rigg), a catsuit-wearing martial arts–trained agent whose husband (Peter) was missing.

From the beginning of season four to the first episode of season seven, John Steed and Mrs. Peel go undercover to investigate all sorts of bizarre situations. During the first episode of season seven, Mrs. Peel's husband (who, seen from a distance, is dressed much like Steed, bowler hat and umbrella and all) returns, and Emma leaves. Tara King (Linda Thorson) becomes his new partner. The show wasn't renewed after that season. Macnee reprised his role as Steed in *The New Avengers* (1976 to 1977), with new partners Purdey (Joanna Lumley) and Mike Gambit (Gareth Hunt).

Q: Which two actresses from The Avengers were also Bond girls?

A: Honor Blackman (who played Cathy Gale in seasons two and three of The Avengers) appeared in the 1964 James Bond movie *Goldfinger* as the memorably named Pussy Galore.

Diana Rigg (Mrs. Emma Peel from seasons four through six and one episode of season seven of The Avengers) appeared in the 1969 James Bond film *On Her Majesty's Secret Service* as the quite tamely named Tracy. Joanna Lumley, who later costarred in *The New Avengers* series, also made a brief appearance in *On Her Majesty's Secret Service*.

The unsuggestive name of the main Bond girl wasn't the only unusual thing about this installment in the James Bond franchise. For more, see the next entry.

Q: Which actor is the lone person to play agent 007 only once in a film in the main Bond franchise?

A: Sean Connery, Roger Moore, Timothy Dalton, Pierce Brosnan, and, most recently, Daniel Craig all played James Bond in multiple films. But one actor has the distinction of only playing agent 007 in a single film: George Lazenby, who appeared as everyone's favorite shaken-not-stirred, martini-drinking super spy in the 1969 film *On Her Majesty's Secret Service* and never again graced the screen as Bond.

Lazenby wasn't a trained actor when he got the role. He was a car mechanic turned used car salesman from Goulburn, Australia. He bought cars from embassy employees and got invited to their parties, which gave him an in (and some insight) into the higher-class diplomatic circles. He followed the girl he loved to London and while working as a car salesman there was scouted and became a successful model. He did some commercial work, but no other acting.

A friend thought he'd be good for Bond, and she convinced him to go to an audition. According to Lazenby himself, he wasn't on the list, so he called the friend back and she told him to get in there somehow. According to Lazenby, he went to Sean Connery's hair stylist for a cut, went to Sean Connery's tailor and stole a suit that Mr. Connery hadn't picked up, and went back to the audition spot, running past the receptionist into the office. He lied about past acting experience and was granted a meeting with the director, to whom he fessed up. But the director was impressed with him, and he got the part.

And he wasn't let go from the series. He was offered a six-picture deal with a hefty (according to him, under-the-table) signing bonus, but he didn't sign the contract. He grew a beard after filming was over, and the studio didn't allow him to go on the publicity tour. On *The Tonight Show with Johnny Carson*, he said he didn't want to do another film, and that was it for his instant stardom. He went into real estate and, although he did continue to pick up roles here and there and is still acting to this day, he has never landed another major Hollywood picture.

The film was also unusual in the series for following the book more closely and for the serious tone of its ending. Bond rescues the Contessa Teresa "Tracy" di Vicenzo (played by Diana Rigg) from a suicide attempt. She turns out to be the daughter of mob boss Marc-Ange Draco. Draco tries to convince Bond to marry or date Tracy and offers a dowry of a million pounds. Bond says he's more interested in the whereabouts of his longtime nemesis Ernst Stavro Blofeld (played by Telly Savalas). The usual 007 hijinks ensue. Bond falls in love and intends to live happily ever after with Tracy, until tragedy strikes in the end. Lazenby was nominated for a Golden Globe (New Star of the Year), and the movie was a box-office hit.

One additional actor also could have made a claim to playing Bond once. In the parody film *Casino Royale* (1967), David Niven plays retired agent 007, now Sir James Bond. But this comedic sendup of the genre is not considered an entry in the proper Bond franchise. Ian Fleming's *Casino Royale* got a more serious treatment with the *Casino Royale* film released in 2006 and starring Daniel Craig as James Bond.

Q: Which real-life secret mission inspired the opening of the movie *Goldfinger*?

A: In the opening of the James Bond movie *Goldfinger*, Bond pops up out of the water near a shore (in a wetsuit, with a fake bird on his head), walks onto a beach, scales a wall with a grappling hook, tussles with a guard, sneaks into what looks like a silo, sets C-4 explosives on tanks of nitro with a timer, walks out, removes his wetsuit to reveal a pristine white tuxedo and black tie, places a flower in his lapel, walks into a party at a bar, and lights a cigarette just as the explosion goes off. It turns out he blew up a heroin factory. The scene wasn't in Ian Fleming's book *Goldfinger*, which started in the bar. It was likely added by British former SOE officer (during WWII) Paul Dehn, who wrote the SEO training manual and was one of the *Goldfinger* screenplay cowriters.

Believe it or not, a good portion of this story really happened, although the setting was quite different. During WWII, two Dutch agents were trapped behind enemy lines in the Netherlands (which was occupied by Nazi Germany). Queen Wilhelmina (under exile in Britain) sent a team of agents to exfiltrate them with help from MI6 agents Peter Tazelaar, Hazelhoff Roelfzema, and Bob Van der Stok. The agents took a British motor gunboat from Britain, disguised it as a dinghy, and rowed along the shore near the Palace Resort at Scheveningen, where the Nazis had set up headquarters and regularly threw parties on Friday nights.

Tazelaar and Roelfzema exited the dinghy and swam to the beach, where Roelfzema helped Tazelaar out of his wetsuit. Underneath, he was wearing a tuxedo. Roelfzema splashed Hennessy XO brandy onto Tazelaar and returned to the dinghy, and Tazelaar proceeded past the guards (who likely assumed he was a wandering partygoer) and into the resort.

The bold entry worked like a charm, but the rest of the mission didn't go so well. First, Tazelaar was apprehended by the Gestapo on his way to a rendezvous with Roelfzema to pick up radio transmitters. He got out of it by continuing to act like a partygoer and offering them some gin, and because a policeman in the resistance vouched for him. Then someone betrayed the Dutch resistance and made it impossible for him to get the two men he was there to rescue out. He escaped alone. He continued doing missions during WWII and during the Dutch colonial war in Indonesia, and eventually became a Europe-based CIA agent in the 1950s.

Q: Which Bond film did not include the iconic theme music or silhouette opening?

A: EON Productions, founded by Albert R. Broccoli and Harry Saltzman, has held the rights to the Bond franchise for decades and made twenty-four 007 films, starting with *Dr. No* starring Sean Connery. After *Diamonds Are Forever* (1971), where Connery reprised his role as Bond after George Lazenby refused to do the next picture, Connery said he'd never do another Bond movie. His replacement for the next few installments was Roger Moore.

In the late 1950s, Ivar Bryce partnered with Kevin McClory to produce a film of McClory's. Bryce introduced McClory to his friend Ian Fleming with the aim of developing a Bond film next. McClory didn't think the existing stories were cinematic enough, so he, Fleming, and a screenwriter named Jack Whittingham collaborated on a new story that Whittingham turned into a first-draft screenplay. But the project went nowhere.

Ian Fleming incorporated some of the ideas from the collaboration into his novel *Thunderball* and failed to credit anyone else. Lawsuits for credit and damages ensued. In 1963, McClory received a settlement and the rights to the *Thunderball* screen treatments. (Whittingham dropped out of the case due to financial difficulties and got nothing). Fleming suffered several heart attacks during the proceedings. He died in 1964.

McClory was listed as a producer on the 1965 film *Thunderball*.

In the 1980s, he decided he wanted to make the original story into a movie. His team approached Sean Connery with an offer of $5 million, plus a share of the profits. He said yes, and *Never Say Never Again* (an apparent joke about Connery's "never" comment) was born. The movie was directed by Irvin Kershner (director of *The Empire Strikes Back*).

Because the producers didn't have the rights to the rest of the Bond franchise outside of the one story, they couldn't use the iconic Bond theme music and couldn't reprise the opening where Connery spins and shoots at the camera in silhouette. Also, Q was called Algernon. But Connery was once again playing Bond, this time with some humorous cracks about his status as an aging spy.

Q: Which Cold War–era television show featured an American and a Russian agent working together to fight evildoers?

A: The spy show *The Man from U.N.C.L.E.* ran from 1964 to 1968. It featured Robert Vaughn as American Napoleon Solo and David McCallum as Russian Illya Kuryakin, both agents of the United Network Command for Law Enforcement (U.N.C.L.E.). They usually thwarted the plans of an organization of villains with a name that was even more of a mouthful than their own: the Technological Hierarchy for the Removal of Undesirables and the Subjugation of Humanity (T.H.R.U.S.H.).

The show had a one-season spinoff called *The Girl from U.N.C.L.E.*, which ran from 1966 to 1967, with Stefanie Powers as U.N.C.L.E. agent April Dancer.

And a movie, *The Man from U.N.C.L.E.*, was released in 2015, directed by Guy Ritchie.

A : Kim Philby (née Harold Philby) was a member of the Cambridge Five, a group of friends who were recruited by the Soviets during their time at university in the early 1930s. In 1936, during the Spanish Civil War, Philby went to Spain posing as a journalist, but he was actually spying for Russia. He was caught by Franco's men while in possession of Russian message encoding instructions, written on rice paper. At the police station, he distracted his captors by throwing his wallet and quickly ate the paper.

The Cambridge Five was tasked by their Russian handlers with infiltrating British intelligence. The group, especially Philby, rose to great heights in MI6 and other intelligence branches and remained there for decades.

After he was found out, Philby fled to Russia. In 1968, he published *My Silent War*, a memoir explaining his motivations, including loyalty to the cause of communism, which he thought would win out over democracy. Journalist Phillip Knightley interviewed Philby for days in Russia shortly before he died, and the only hint of regret Knightley noted was at the mention of Julius and Ethel Rosenberg. They and other Russian spies in the American nuclear program had been found out with the help of the Venona Decrypts. To hide the fact that there was a high-level mole, Philby was ordered to warn only the most important of Russia's agents. The Rosenbergs were among the ones given no warning and no chance to flee. No one expected them to be put to death, but they were convicted and executed by electric chair.

Whittaker Chambers (née J. Vivian Chambers) was from Philadelphia. He joined the Communist Party of the United States of America, and a few years later, in 1931, became a courier of secret documents between Soviet spies and their handlers. Unlike with Philby, Stalin's purges and the 1939 pact between the Nazis and Soviet Russia prompted him to switch sides. Chambers gave information about Russia's spy network to Assistant Secretary of State Adolf Berle, who initially didn't believe the tidbit that one of his own people, Alger Hiss, was a mole (Alger Hiss had been brought by FDR to a postwar meeting in Yalta between FDR, Churchill, and Stalin in 1945). In the 1950s, Chambers again mentioned that Hiss was a spy, this time in front of the House Un-American Activities Committee, where he was taken more seriously. In 1952, Chambers put out his memoir *Witness*, explaining his motivations to spy for the Soviets, but after he had already turned away from them.

Historians would caution you to take these memoirs with a grain of salt, although Graham Greene seemed to take Philby at his word, according to his foreword to *My Silent War*.

A : Author W. Somerset Maugham was a spy for Britain during WWI. He spoke German and French and his book, *Of Human Bondage*, had come out in 1915. Already being a well-known author gave him a cover. He went to Switzerland as a spy in neutral territory, and then to Russia. He later wrote *Ashendon: or The British Agent*, published in 1928, a collection of stories about Ashendon, a shy bookish spy who worked as a cog at a bureaucracy. The book portrayed both the routine and exciting work and the moral ambiguity involved in the profession.

Graham Greene was born in 1904 and studied at Oxford. He worked at MI6, and Kim Philby (the famous Cambridge Five mole) was his friend and handler. Graham Greene wrote the preface to the British edition of Kim Philby's autobiography *My Silent War*.

In Greene's novel *Our Man in Havana* (1958), a down-on-his-luck British vacuum salesman in Havana named James Wormold is recruited by MI6 because they need someone local. He becomes agent 59200/5. But rather than doing any real spy work, he fakes a spy ring and makes up reports, sometimes using real names of people in the area, and sends drawings of vacuum cleaner parts that are purportedly diagrams of military installations. Then, the people mentioned in his reports start dying. *Our Man in Havana* was made into a movie and released in 1959, with Alec Guinness as Wormold.

Dashiell Hammett is best known for writing famous detective novels turned into movies, like *The Maltese Falcon* (which featured famous fictional detective Sam Spade) and *The Thin Man* (with rich social butterflies Nick and Nora Charles solving crimes). But he also wrote a recurring character called the Continental Op, a pudgy, middle-aged, but effective operative who, like a good spy, never divulges his name. Hammett himself was an operative for the Pinkerton National Detective Agency from 1915 to 1918 and from 1920 to 1922.

John le Carré (pseudonym for David Cornwell) was born in 1931. His father was a con artist. Le Carré attended Oxford, after which he taught Latin and French at Eaton. Then he joined MI5. He transferred to MI6 and did undercover work in West Germany until 1963, when he published his first spy novel, *The Spy Who Came In from the Cold*. In the novel, Alec Leamas is enlisted in a scheme to undermine East German intelligence to get out a much less moral spy named Mundt, a mole for Britain. In another of his well-known works, *Tinker Tailor Soldier Spy* (1974), George Smiley, a retired counterintelligence agent, is brought back to look for a mole, only to find many, including the ringleader, Bill Haydon, who many think is based on Kim Philby. A theme of betrayal persists, which is understandable since le Carré worked at MI6 while the mole ring was still active and got to see the fallout of their discovery firsthand.

Ian Lancaster Fleming, born in 1908, grew up well off and went to Eton and the Royal Military Academy at Sandhurst. He wanted to join the Foreign Service but didn't get accepted. He worked as a journalist and stockbroker. In 1939, he worked for naval intelligence in Room 39 of the Old London Admiralty Building (right next to Room 40, where the cryptology department decoded the Zimmerman Telegram during WWI; see page 94). Fleming came up with plans for covert operations but didn't get to be involved directly. He returned to journalism after the war and wrote *Casino Royale* while on vacation in Jamaica in 1952 (published in 1953). Unlike the movie version, in the novels, Bond wasn't as attractive but was trained to kill. The name James Bond was reportedly the name of an author of a Jamaican bird-watching guide that Fleming had with him. (Read other theories on where the name came from on page 245). By the time Fleming died, his books had sold over 4 million copies.

Q: What novel prompted Britain to examine its coastal defenses?

A: In Erskine Childers's novel *The Riddle of the Sands*, published in 1903, the protagonists (who are not professional spies) decide to go on a quest to demonstrate that Britain is vulnerable to a naval attack from Kaiser Wilhelm II's Germany. They pilot a small boat to Germany and do, indeed, overhear German plans to invade Britain. The popular novel prompted Britain to reevaluate its coastal defenses.

Childers also holds the distinction of becoming a spy after writing spy fiction rather than before. He was a member of the British Special Forces during World War II.

Q: Which actor and show creator fled his country over responses to his spy show's finale?

A: Patrick McGoohan created and starred in the 1967 to 1968 hit spy TV show *The Prisoner*. In the show, the character tendered his resignation at a British intelligence agency, and rather than being allowed to leave, he was kidnapped and imprisoned in a strange and unknown location—a town populated by people who seemed to be fellow spies, and where everyone insisted on calling him Number 6. Number 2, the apparent leader, foiled his escape plans weekly, sometimes with the help of white, balloon-like sci-fi sentries.

The show's final episode was a psychedelic trip that departed from the tone of the previous episodes in many ways. The ending also baffled many people. Mr. McGoohan told an interviewer that he and his family had to leave England because the response to the finale left them no privacy. Perhaps the episode title was prescient: "Fallout."

McGoohan also played the lead role in an earlier spy show titled *Secret Agent*, and he played a murderous CIA agent in a 1975 episode of *Columbo* titled "Identity Crisis."

Q: What fake Hollywood studio was set up to help get six American embassy employees out of Tehran?

A: In January and February 1979, the Shah of Iran, Mohammad Reza Pahlavi, was ousted, and the Ayatollah Khomeini took over the country. In October, protesting college students stormed the American embassy, and over fifty embassy employees were taken hostage, interrogated by the revolutionary guard, and in some cases, tortured. A CIA agent at the embassy and some others had shredded thousands of documents before the takeover, and Iranian officials put people to work piecing them back together. Via the documents and interrogation, they got names of agents, employees, and informants, leading to arrests and executions.

Diplomatic efforts to negotiate the release of the hostages failed. The UN Security Council tried to institute economic sanctions, but Russia vetoed them. President Carter's attempted military rescue (operation Eagle Claw) also failed due to helicopter issues, leaving eight soldiers dead and several wounded. The hostages were held for 444 days, until Iran released them on January 20, 1981, the day of the inauguration of President Reagan. Many refer to this series of events as the Iranian hostage crisis.

But on the day the embassy was stormed, six employees had escaped. The visa office had its own entrance and exit, and thirteen staffers fled the building in an attempt to get to the British embassy before the protestors got to them. Outside, the group got split up, and all but six were captured immediately.

The remaining group, including Mark and Cora Lijek, managed to get in touch with Victor Tomseth, deputy chief of mission, the second-highest-ranking US diplomat in Tehran. Tomseth himself was ultimately captured and placed with the hostages, but before that, he called his friend Somchai Sriweawnetr (known as Sam), the US embassy chef from Thailand, and asked him to hide the six fugitives. Sam took them to a safe house, where they hid until it wasn't considered safe anymore. Per Sam, they got out two hours before authorities came to the safe house looking for them.

The six were taken to the house of Canada's chief immigration officer, M. John Vernon Sheardown, and his wife, Zena. They hosted the escapees for eighty-five days while Canada and the US tried to work out how to extract them safely.

The CIA sent Tony Mendez from their technical support division. He was an expert in exfiltration, disguises, and forgery. He'd studied on movie sets and worked with costume and prop makers for help on CIA missions in the past. But this time, he went bigger. He created a whole fake movie studio called Studio Six Productions (six because of the number of the escapees). The plan was to pretend the six plus Mendez were a group of movie location scouts from Canada. He called a Hollywood makeup artist he knew for help finding a screenplay. The makeup artist had been attached to a sci-fi project whose production had fizzled. The script was called *Lord of Light*, written by Barry Ira Geller, based on the Roger Zelazny novel of the same name. It included a Middle Eastern bazaar scene, which was perfect for the cover story. Mendez took the script and renamed it *Argo*.

The CIA rented an office in Los Angeles (last occupied by Michael Douglas) and set up phones in case anyone named Mendez put articles and ads in *Variety* and the *Hollywood Reporter*. (One of the items he carried with him to Tehran as pocket litter was a copy of the *Hollywood Reporter* with one of the ads, along with other items like movie studio business cards and the *Argo* script.) It seemed like a real studio, and people even began sending in scripts—including Stephen Spielberg!

Canada made official Canadian passports with aliases for the six, and Mendez forged visa papers. Mendez flew into Tehran on January 25, 1980. He worked with the group on their cover stories for three days, and they went to the airport for an early-morning flight on the 28th. They lucked out in that the passport agent didn't check their visa papers against copies that were supposed to be kept when people entered the country. One was questioned about his passport photo, but they were ultimately allowed through. After a brief flight delay, they took off for Zurich and freedom.

The CIA's involvement in the exfiltration of the group was kept secret, and it was attributed to only Canadian efforts, but the mission was declassified in the late 1990s. In 2012, a movie titled *Argo* opened in theaters, dramatizing the already-dramatic escape.

Q: What espionage thriller was made for a religious network?

A: Slick Cold War–era thriller *Granite Flats* premiered in 2013. Set in the early 1960s, it features Soviet satellites, G-men, and Project MK-ULTRA mind-control drugs (a real CIA program; see page 201)—all real-world Cold War stuff wrapped into a period drama that revolves around a small town, a military base, and a group of kids who live there.

It probably sounds like a typical period drama, but the unique thing about *Granite Flats* is that it was made specifically for Brigham Young University's TV network BYUtv, with the aim of providing quality entertaining programming that doesn't contain profanity, nudity, too much violence, and other things antithetical to the Mormon religion. But it also accomplishes this without being overtly religious.

CONCLUSION

All of the above is the tip of the iceberg. Our intelligence agencies have undertaken covert operations in the US and all over the world. And so, of course, have other countries' intelligence services. And localities. And companies. And individuals.

There were so many things I wanted to include but didn't have time to. One thing still in the news as of this writing is the documented Russian interference in the US election in 2016. Hopefully, journalists, historians, and others piece together the true chain of events about that and other covert goings-on.

In our digital age, revelations are coming faster and faster, especially with most of us carrying around an incredible new-fangled surveillance device—the smartphone. At the time of this writing, protests have broken out all over the US (and throughout the world) over the horrific killing of George Floyd by a Minneapolis police officer (caught on camera), as well as a spate of other extrajudicial killings of unarmed African Americans that finally sparked mass outrage. The killing of jogger Ahmaud Arbery in Brunswick, Georgia, didn't result in an arrest until two months later, when cellphone footage of the incident went public. Some acts of potential provocation during the protests have been caught, too. And lots of moments of everyday racism. Hopefully, this new citizen surveillance capability will prove to be a force for change.

I hope that you found this information both entertaining and illuminating, and that it whets your appetite for other materials on the subject. The reference section is a good place to start. There is a lot of great stuff out there, including books written by spies themselves and material in declassified documents on the FBI and CIA websites. And, if you don't feel like reading more about it, documentaries abound. I, for one, will continue to study our hidden history, keep tabs on past events as they become declassified, and, of course, watch and read spy entertainment.

May you never get caught up in the great game.

REFERENCES

"Afghanistan: The Soviet Union's Vietnam." AlJazeera.com. Last modified April 23, 2003. https://www.aljazeera.com/archive/2003/04/2008410113842420760.html.

"Agent Garbo." Security Service MI5. Accessed October 14, 2020. https://www.mi5.gov.uk/agent-garbo.

"Alexander Litvinenko: Profile of Murdered Russian Spy." BBC.com. January 21, 2016. https://www.bbc.com/news/uk-19647226.

Allen, Thomas B. *George Washington, Spymaster: How the Americans Outspied the British and Won the Revolutionary War*. Washington, D.C.: National Geographic Society, 2004.

Allen, Thomas B. *Harriet Tubman, Secret Agent: How Daring Slaves and Free Blacks Spied for the Union during the Civil War*. Washington, D.C.: National Geographic Society, 2009.

Anderson, Jack and Joseph Spear. "Mata Hari Was Framed, Files Show." *The Washington Post*. November 23, 1985. CIA declassified December 22, 2011. https://www.cia.gov/library/readingroom/document/cia-rdp90-00965r000100120015-5.

Andrew, Professor Christopher. "The Rise of the Islamist Terrorist Threat." Security Service MI5. Accessed October 11, 2020. https://www.mi5.gov.uk/the-rise-of-the-islamist-terrorist-threat

"The Arab-Israeli War of 1948." US Department of State Office of the Historian. Accessed October 11, 2020. https://history.state.gov/milestones/1945-1952/arab-israeli-war.

"Arthur Zimmermann." *Encyclopaedia Britannica*. Last modified June 2, 2020. https://www.britannica.com/biography/Arthur-Zimmermann.

Atwood, Margaret. *The Testaments*. Read by Derek Jacobi, Mae Whitman, Ann Dowd, Bryce Dallas Howard, Tantoo Cardinal, and Margaret Atwood. New York: Nan A. Talese, 2019. Audible audio ed., 13 hours, 18 minutes.

The Avengers (1961). IMDb. Accessed June 16, 2020. https://www.imdb.com/title/tt0054518.

Basilica di San Marco. "St. Mark the Evangelist—Theft." n.d. Accessed
    June 26, 2020. http://www.basilicasanmarco.it/storia-e-societa
    /san-marco-evangelista/il-trafugamento/?lang=en.
"Battle of Saratoga." History.com. Last modified January 14, 2020.
    https://www.history.com/topics/american-revolution/battle-of
    -saratoga.
Bergen, Peter. "September 11 Attacks." *Encyclopaedia Britannica*. Last
    modified September 10, 2020. https://www.britannica.com/event
    /September-11-attacks.
Bernstein, Carl and Bob Woodward. *All the President's Men*. Read by
    Richard Poe. New York: Simon & Schuster, 2012. Audible audio ed.,
    12 hours, 55 minutes.
"Beta Israel." *Encyclopaedia Britannica*. Last modified January 12, 2019.
    https://www.britannica.com/topic/Beta-Israel.
Beyer, Rick, dir. *The Ghost Army*. 2013; Seattle, WA: Amazon Prime,
    2013.
Bhattacharjee, Yudhijit. "A New Kind of Spy." *The New Yorker*. April 28,
    2014. https://www.newyorker.com/magazine/2014/05/05/a-new
    -kind-of-spy.
Bhattacharjee, Yudhijit. "How the FBI Cracked a Chinese Spy Ring."
    The New Yorker. May 12, 2014. https://www.newyorker.com/news
    /news-desk/how-the-f-b-i-cracked-a-chinese-spy-ring/amp.
"Boeing Punished for Spying." BBC News. Last modified July 24, 2003.
    http://news.bbc.co.uk/2/hi/business/3094825.stm.
Born, Matt. "Le Carre to Reveal His Secret Past as a Spy." *The
    Telegraph*. December 9, 2000. https://www.telegraph.co.uk/news
    /uknews/1377589/Le-Carre-to-reveal-his-secret-past-as-a-spy.html.
Bowcott, Owen. "How Fate, and Stalin, Finally Dealt the 'Ace of Spies,'
    A Losing Hand." *The Guardian*. September 7, 2002. https://www
    .theguardian.com/uk/2002/sep/07/russia.artsandhumanities.
Bowermaster, David. "Boeing Probe Intensifies over Secret Lockheed
    Papers." *Seattle Times*. January 9, 2005. https://www.seattletimes
    .com/business/boeing-probe-intensifies-over-secret-lockheed
    -papers.

Brook, Pete. "Inside the Infamous Stasi Prison." *Wired*. October 12, 2010. https://www.wired.com/2010/10/phillip-lohoefener.

"Bunker Tours." Greenbier.com. Accessed June 25, 2020. https://www.greenbrier.com/Activities-Events/Bunker-Tours-(10).aspx.

Burton, Kristen D. "Siren of the Resistance: The Artistry and Espionage of Josephine Baker." NationalWW2Museum.org. February 1, 2020. https://www.nationalww2museum.org/war/articles/siren-resistance -artistry-and-espionage-josephine-baker.

Caesar, Julius. *The Gallic Wars*. n.d. Accessed June 25, 2020. http://classics.mit.edu/Caesar/gallic.mb.txt.

Casino Royale (1967). IMDb. Accessed June 16, 2020. https://www.imdb.com/title/tt0061452.

Casino Royale (2006). IMDb. Accessed June 21, 2020. https://www.imdb.com/title/tt0381061.

Cavanaugh, Ray. "Mata Hari's True Story Remains a Mystery 100 Years After Her Death." *Time*. October 13, 2017. https://time.com/4977634 /mata-hari-true-history.

Charlie Wilson's War (2007). IMDb. Accessed June 21, 2020. https://www.imdb.com/title/tt0472062.

Churton, Tobias. *Aleister Crowley in America: Art, Espionage, and Sex Magick in the New World*. Rochester, VT: Inner Traditions, 2017.

Cochrane, Kira. "What Made the Red Sea Sharks Attack?" *The Guardian*. December 7, 2010. https://www.theguardian.com/world /2010/dec/07/what-made-sharks-attack.

"COINTELPRO." FBI.gov. Accessed September 25, 2020. https://vault.fbi.gov/cointel-pro.

Coleman, Janet Wyman. *Secrets, Lies, Gizmos, and Spies: A History of Spies and Espionage*. New York: Abrams Books for Young Readers, 2006.

"Collapse of the Soviet Union." *Encyclopaedia Britannica*. Last modified August 11, 2020. https://www.britannica.com/event/the -collapse-of-the-Soviet-Union/Aftermath-of-the-coup#ref1258664.

Columbo. "Identity Crisis." 1975. Accessed July 5, 2020. https://www .imdb.com/title/tt0072804.

Conrad, Joseph. *The Secret Agent*. England: Oxford University Press, 2004.

Correll, John T. "Hitler's Buzz Bombs." *Air Force Magazine*. March 1, 2020. https://www.airforcemag.com/article/hitlers-buzz-bombs.

Cowell, Alan. "Overlooked No More: Alan Turing, Condemned Code Breaker and Computer Visionary." *The New York Times*. June 5, 2019. https://www.nytimes.com/2019/06/05/obituaries/alan-turing-overlooked.html.

"Creation of Israel, 1948." US Department of State Office of the Historian. Accessed October 11, 2020. https://history.state.gov/milestones/1945-1952/creation-israel.

Dasgupta, Aditya. "Crateology?" Foreign Policy. August 23, 2006. https://foreignpolicy.com/2006/08/23/crateology.

Debruge, Peter. "Revisiting 1983's 'Never Say Never Again.'" *Variety*. August 24, 2012. https://variety.com/2012/film/reviews/revisiting-1983-s-never-say-never-again-1118058278/amp.

"Department of Near Eastern Antiquities." The Louvre Museum. Accessed October 11, 2020. https://www.louvre.fr/en/departments/near-eastern-antiquities.

Diebel, Anne. "Dashiell Hammett's Strange Career." TheParisReview.org. September 14, 2018. https://www.theparisreview.org/blog/2018/09/14/dashiell-hammetts-strange-career.

Economic Espionage Act of 1996. October 11, 1996. https://www.govinfo.gov/content/pkg/PLAW-104publ294/pdf/PLAW-104publ294.pdf.

"Egypt Killed Wrong Sharks after Diver Attacks: NGO." Reuters. December 4, 2010. https://www.reuters.com/article/us-egypt-sharks-idUSTRE6B31KX20101204.

"Exotic Dancer and Spy Mata Hari Is Executed." History.com. November 24, 2009. Accessed October 14, 2020. https://www.history.com/this-day-in-history/mata-hari-executed.

"Faysal I." *Encyclopaedia Britannica*. Last updated September 4, 2020. https://www.britannica.com/biography/Faysal-I.

"FBI Founded." History.com. July 21, 2010. Accessed July 5, 2020.
https://www.history.com/this-day-in-history/fbi-founded.

Félix, Doreen St. "The Haunted Image of Harriet Tubman on the
Twenty-Dollar Bill." *The New Yorker*. June 18, 2019. https://www
.newyorker.com/culture/cultural-comment/the-haunted-image-of
-harriet-tubman-on-the-twenty-dollar-bill.

Fialka, John J. "How the Secrets Moved East." *Air Force Magazine*.
April 1, 1997. https://www.airforcemag.com/article/0497secrets.

Fisher, Max. "Saudis Declare Vulture Innocent of Espionage."
The Atlantic. January 11, 2011. https://www.theatlantic.com
/international/archive/2011/01/saudis-declare-vulture-innocent
-of-espionage/339208.

Fitzgibbon, Sinead. 2013. *The Gunpowder Plot: History in an Hour*.
Read by Jonathan Keeble. New York: Harper Collins. 1 hour,
4 minutes.

"Francis Gary Powers." *Encyclopaedia Britannica*. Last modified April 6,
2020. https://www.britannica.com/biography/Francis-Gary-Powers.

Frederique, Nadine. 2016. "COINTELPRO." *Encyclopaedia Britannica*.
Last modified December 17, 2018. https://www.britannica.com/topic
/COINTELPRO.

Freedman, Samuel G. "Pop Culture and Religious Sensibility on a
Mormon TV Network." *The New York Times*. October 31, 2014.
https://www.nytimes.com/2014/11/01/us/a-formula-for-pop-culture
-and-religious-sensibility-on-a-mormon-tv-network.html.

Friedersdorf, Conor. "The Secret Story of How the NSA Began." *The
Atlantic*. November 27, 2013. https://www.theatlantic.com/politics
/archive/2013/11/the-secret-story-of-how-the-nsa-began/281862.

Galvin, Andrews. "Boeing to Settle Charges." *The Orange County
Register*. May 15, 2006. https://www.ocregister.com/2006/05/15
/boeing-to-settle-charges.

Garber, Megan. "Ghost Army: The Inflatable Tanks That Fooled
Hitler." *The Atlantic*. May 22, 2013. http://www.theatlantic.com/amp
/article/276137.

Gardner, Robert H., dir. *Enemy of the Reich: The Noor Inayat Khan Story*. 2014. PBS. Seattle: WA. Amazon Prime, 55 minutes.

"Giacomo Casanova." *Encyclopaedia Britannica*. Last modified May 31, 2020. https://www.britannica.com/biography/Giacomo-Casanova.

Giaimo, Cara. "One of the Earliest Industrial Spies Was a French Missionary Stationed in China." AtlasObscura.com. April 28, 2017. https://www.atlasobscura.com/articles/porcelain-corporate-espionage-china-missionary-dentrecolles.

The Girl from U.N.C.L.E. (1966). IMDb. Accessed June 16, 2020. https://www.imdb.com/title/tt0059988.

Greenbaum, Josh, dir. *Becoming Bond*. 2017. Los Angeles, CA: Delirio Films. 95 minutes.

Greenberg, Richard, Paul Cruickshank, and Chris Hansen. "Inside the Terror Plot That 'Rivaled 9/11.'" NBC News. September 15, 2008. http://www.nbcnews.com/id/26726987/ns/dateline_nbc-the_hansen_files_with_chris_hansen/t/inside-terror-plot-rivaled.

Goldfinger (1964). IMDb. Accessed June 16, 2020. https://www.imdb.com/title/tt0058150.

Granite Flats (2013–2016). IMDb. Accessed June 25, 2020. https://www.imdb.com/title/tt2624370.

Hamilton, Robert E. "1983: The Year of Living Dangerously." FPRI.org. December 3, 2018. https://www.fpri.org/article/2018/12/able-archer-at-35-lessons-of-the-1983-war-scare.

Hanson, Jason. *Spy Secrets That Can Save Your Life*. New York: TarcherPerigee, 2016.

Harrison, David. "The Secret War Mission That Inspired Goldfinger Scene." *The Telegraph*. April 17, 2010. https://www.telegraph.co.uk/news/newstopics/howaboutthat/7601274/The-secret-war-mission-that-inspired-Goldfinger-scene.html.

Hasic, Albinko. "See the 'Loose Lips Sink Ships' Propaganda Posters of World War II." *Time*. December 8, 2016. https://time.com/4591841/loose-lips-sink-ships-posters.

Heiligenstein, Michael X. "A Brief History of the NSA: From 1917 to 2014." *The Saturday Evening Post*. April 17, 2014. https://www .saturdayeveningpost.com/2014/04/a-brief-history-of-the-nsa.

Herodotus. *The History of Herodotus Vol. II*. Translated by G. C. Macauley. http://www.gutenberg.org/files/2456/2456-h/2456-h.htm.

Higgitt, Rebekah. "The Real Story of the Secret Agent and the Greenwich Observatory Bombing." *The Guardian*. August 5, 2016. https://www.google.com/amp/s/amp.theguardian.com/science /the-h-word/2016/aug/05/secret-agent-greenwich-observatory -bombing-of-1894.

Hill, James, dir. *The Avengers*. Season 7, Episode 1, "The Forget-Me-Knot." Aired March 20, 1968, ITV.

Hitz, Frederick Porter. *The Great Game: The Myth and Reality of Espionage*. New York: Alfred A. Knopf, 2004.

"Ho Chi Minh." *Encyclopaedia Britannica*. Last modified March 30, 2020. https://www.history.com/topics/vietnam-war/ho-chi-minh-1

"Interview with Paul Fritz Bugas." PBS.org. Accessed October 11, 2020. https://www.pbs.org/wgbh/americanexperience/features /bomb-interview.

Jacobsen, Annie. "Intelligence in Public Literature - Operation Paperclip: The Secret Intelligence Program to bring Nazi Scientists to America." CIA.gov. October 6, 2014. https://www.cia.gov/library /center-for-the-study-of-intelligence/csi-publications/csi-studies /studies/vol-58-no-3/operation-paperclip-the-secret-intelligence -program-to-bring-nazi-scientists-to-america.html.

"James Bond." Eon.co.uk. Accessed June 25, 2020. https://www.eon .co.uk/james-bond.

"Japanese Internment Camps." History.com. Last modified February 21, 2020. https://www.history.com/topics/world-war-ii/japanese -american-relocation.

Jagernauth, Kevin. "Steven Spielberg Sent a Script to the Fake Movie Studio the CIA Set Up to Make 'Argo,' Was It 'E.T.'?" *Indie Wire*. October 16, 2012. https://www.indiewire.com/2012/10/steven

-spielberg-sent-a-script-to-the-fake-movie-studio-the-cia-set-up
-to-make-argo-was-it-e-t-250767/amp.

"John le Carré." *Encyclopaedia Britannica*. Last modified October 22,
2019. https://www.britannica.com/biography/John-le-Carre.

Jordan, Borimir. "The Ceremony of the Helots in Thucydides, IV, 80."
L'Antiquité Classique 59 (1990): 37–69. Accessed October 11, 2020.
http://www.jstor.org/stable/41655694.

"Joseph McCarthy." *Encyclopaedia Britannica*. Last modified April 28,
2020. https://www.britannica.com/biography/Joseph-McCarthy.

"Josephine Baker." *Encyclopaedia Britannica*. Last modified May 30,
2020. https://www.britannica.com/biography/Josephine-Baker.

Kapelrud, Arvid S. "Aaron." *Encyclopaedia Britannica*. Last modified
June 6, 2011. https://www.britannica.com/biography/Aaron-biblical
-figure.

Kautilya. *Arthashastra*. Translated by R. Shamasastry. Archives.org.
Accessed September 24, 2020. https://archive.org/details
/Arthashastra_Of_Chanakya__Other_Books/page/n585/mode
/2up.

Kayyali, Dia. "The History of Surveillance and the Black Community."
EFF.org. February 13, 2014. https://www.eff.org/deeplinks/2014/02
/history-surveillance-and-black-community.

Keller, Werner and Joachim Rohork. *The Bible as History*. New York:
William Morrow Paperbacks, 2015.

Kessler, Glenn. "The Iraq War and WMDs: An Intelligence Failure or
White House Spin?" *The Washington Post*. March 22, 2019. https://
www.washingtonpost.com/politics/2019/03/22/iraq-war-wmds
-an-intelligence-failure-or-white-house-spin.

The King James Version of the Bible. n.d. Project Gutenberg. https://
www.gutenberg.org/files/10/10-h/10-h.htm.

Kipling, Rudyard. *Kim*. 1901. https://www.gutenberg.org/files/2226/2226
-h/2226-h.htm.

"KKK Series." FBI.gov. Accessed September 25, 2020. https://www.fb
i.gov/history/famous-cases/kkk-series.

Knell, Yolande. "Shark Attacks Not Linked to Mossad, Says Israel." BBC
News. December 7, 2010. https://www.bbc.com/news/world-middle
-east-11937285.

Krayenbuhl, Sabine and Zeva Oelbaum, dirs. *Letters from Baghdad*.
2016; United States: Letters from Baghdad, LTD/Between The Rivers
Productions, LLC, 2018. Amazon Prime, 96 minutes.

Krebs, A.V. "Bitter Harvest." *The Washington Post*. February 2, 1992.
https://www.washingtonpost.com/archive/opinions/1992/02/02
/bitter-harvest/c8389b23-884d-43bd-ad34-bf7b11077135/?tid=a
_classic-iphone&p9w22b2p=b2p22p9w00098&no_nav=true.

Landau, Elizabeth. "What Polonium Does to the Body." CNN. Last
modified November 29, 2012. https://www.cnn.com/2012/11/27
/health/polonium-arafat-explainer/index.html.

Lane, Megan. "Operation Mincemeat: How a Dead Tramp Fooled
Hitler." BBC News. December 3, 2010. https://www.bbc.com/news
/magazine-11887115.

Laurie, Clayton D. "Studies in Intelligence: CIA and the Wars in
Southeast Asia 1947-75." *Journal of the American Intelligence
Professional*. September 2016. https://www.cia.gov/library/center
-for-the-study-of-intelligence/csi-publications/books-and-mono
graphs/Anthology-CIA-and-the-Wars-in-Southeast-Asia/pdfs-1
/vietnam-anthology-interactive.pdf.

Leveen, Lois. "Mary Richards Bowser (fl. 1846–1867)." *Encyclopedia
Virginia*. Last modified March 6, 2018. https://www.encyclopedia
virginia.org/Bowser_Mary_Richards_fl_1846-1867#start_entry.

Leveen, Lois. "She Was Born Into Slavery, Was a Spy and Is Celebrated
as a Hero—But We're Missing the Point of the 'Mary Bowser' Story."
Time. Last modified June 19, 2019. https://time.com/5609045
/misremembering-mary-bowser.

Lewis, Gareth, dir. *Spy Wars with Damian Lewis*. Season 1, Episode
1, "The Man Who Saved the World." Aired October 7, 2019,
Smithsonian Channel. Amazon Prime.

Lewis, Gareth, dir. *Spy Wars with Damian Lewis*. Season 1, Episode 2. "Bombs in the Sky." Aired October 14, 2019, Smithsonian Channel. Amazon Prime.

Lewis, Gareth, dir. *Spy Wars with Damian Lewis*. Season 1, Episode 3. "The Spies Next Door." Aired October 21, 2019, Smithsonian Channel. Amazon Prime.

Lewis, Gareth, dir. *Spy Wars with Damian Lewis*. Season 1, Episode 4. "A Perfect Traitor." Aired October 28, 2019, Smithsonian Channel. Amazon Prime.

Lewis, Gareth, dir. *Spy Wars with Damian Lewis*. Season 1, Episode 5. "Escape from Tehran." Aired November 4, 2019, Smithsonian Channel. Amazon Prime.

Lewis, Gareth, dir. *Spy Wars with Damian Lewis*. Season 1, Episode 6. "Trojan Horse." Aired November 11, 2019, Smithsonian Channel. Amazon Prime.

Lewis, Gareth, dir. *Spy Wars with Damian Lewis*. Season 1, Episode 7. "Merchant of Death." Aired November 18, 2019, Smithsonian Channel. Amazon Prime.

Lewis, Gareth, dir. *Spy Wars with Damian Lewis*. Season 1, Episode 8. "Exodus." Aired November 25, 2019, Smithsonian Channel. Amazon Prime.

Lineberry, Cate. "The Thrilling Tale of How Robert Smalls Seized a Confederate Ship and Sailed it to Freedom." *Smithsonian Magazine*. June 13, 2017. https://www.smithsonianmag.com/history /thrilling-tale-how-robert-smalls-heroically-sailed-stolen-confederate -ship-freedom-180963689.

Liulevicius, Vejas G. *The Great Courses: Espionage and Covert Operations: a Global History*. Chantilly, VA: Teaching Company, 2011.

"Lot 89; The Property of a Gentleman; Mata Hari [Margaretha Geertruida Zelle] (1876–1917), French Spy..." *Christie's*. June 12, 2008. https://www.christies.com/lotfinder/Lot/mata-hari-margaretha- geertruida-zelle-1876-1917-french-5085833-details.aspx

"Louis XV." *Encyclopaedia Britannica*. Last modified May 06, 2020. https://www.britannica.com/biography/Louis-XV.

The Man from U.N.C.L.E. (1964). IMDb. Accessed June 16, 2020. https://www.imdb.com/title/tt0057765.

The Man from U.N.C.L.E. (2015). IMDb. Accessed June 16, 2020. https://www.imdb.com/title/tt1638355.

The Man Who Never Was. (1956). IMDb. Accessed October 11, 2020. https://www.imdb.com/title/tt0049471.

"Manaus." *Encyclopaedia Britannica*. Last modified November 26, 2019. https://www.britannica.com/place/Manaus.

Mansky, Jackie. "The True Story of the Death of Stalin." *Smithsonian Magazine*. October 10, 2017. https://www.smithsonianmag.com /history/true-story-death-stalin-180965119.

"Mata Hari (1876–1917)." Biography. Last modified August 12, 2020. https://www.biography.com/performer/mata-hari.

Mazzetti, Mark. "Burglars Who Took On F.B.I. Abandon Shadows." *The New York Times*. January 7, 2014. https://www.nytimes.com. /2014/01/07/us/burglars-who-took-on-fbi-abandon-shadows.html

McRobbie, Linda Rodriguez. "The Incredible Chevalier d'Eon, Who Left France as a Male Spy and Returned as a Christian Woman." AtlasObscura.com. July 29, 2016. https://www.atlasobscura.com /articles/the-incredible-chevalier-deon-who-left-france-as-a-male -spy-and-returned-as-a-christian-woman.amp.

"Members of the IC." DNI.gov. Accessed June 11 2020. https://www .dni.gov/index.php/what-we-do/members-of-the-ic.

Meyer, Pamela. 2011. "How to Spot a Liar." TEDGlobal. Video, 18:35. https://www.ted.com/talks/pamela_meyer_how_to_spot_a_liar /up-next?language=en.

"Mikhail Gorbachev." *Encyclopaedia Britannica*. Last modified February 27, 2020. https://www.britannica.com/biography/Mikhail-Gorbachev.

Morgan, Thad. "How a Slave-Turned-Spy Helped Secure a Victory at the Battle of Yorktown." History.com. February 4, 2019. https:// www.history.com/.amp/news/battle-of-yorktown-slave-spy-james -armistead.

Myre, Greg. "How the CIA Found A Soviet Sub—Without the Soviets Knowing." NPR.org. September 18, 2017. https://www.npr.org/sections/parallels/2017/09/18/549535352/how-the-cia-found-a-soviet-sub-without-the-soviets-knowing.

Myre, Greg. "'A Woman of No Importance' Finally Gets Her Due." NPR.org. April 18, 2019. https://www.npr.org/2019/04/18/711356336/a-woman-of-no-importance-finally-gets-her-due.

The New Avengers (1976–1977). IMDb. Accessed November 23, 2020. https://www.imdb.com/title/tt0074031.

Newman, Lily Hay. "How to Sweep For Bugs and Hidden Cameras." *Wired*. December 9, 2017. https://www.wired.com/story/how-to-sweep-for-bugs/amp.

Nero, Dom. "The Real Spies Who Inspired James Bond Are Far More Fascinating Than the Big Screen 007s." *Esquire*. January 16, 2020. https://www.esquire.com/entertainment/movies/amp30533681/james-bond-true-story-real-life-inspiration-ian-fleming.

Oi, Mariko. "Japan's Ninjas Heading for Extinction." BBC News. November 23, 2012. https://www.bbc.com/news/magazine-20135674.

Olson, Lynne. "Olson's Portrait of SOE Bravery in WW2 Undone by Incompetence at the Top." *Financial Review*. May 19, 2017. https://www.afr.com/life-and-luxury/arts-and-culture/olsons-portrait-of-soe-bravery-in-ww2-undone-by-incompetence-at-the-top-20170516-gw5pz3.

On Her Majesty's Secret Service. IMDb. Accessed June 16, 2020. https://www.imdb.com/title/tt0064757.

"Operation Mincemeat." Ian Fleming. August 16, 2016. http://www.ianfleming.com/timeline/dieppe-raid.

"Osama bin Laden." *Encyclopaedia Britannica*. Last updated April 28, 2020. https://www.britannica.com/biography/Osama-bin-Laden.

Our Man in Havana. IMDb. Accessed June 23, 2020. https://www.imdb.com/title/tt0054152.

"Palmer Raids." History.com. Last modified August 21, 2018. https://www.history.com/topics/red-scare/palmer-raids.

Paris, Natalie. "Ex-Soviet Spy Given James Bond Honour." *The Telegraph*. October 18, 2007. https://www.telegraph.co.uk/news /uknews/1566585/Ex-Soviet-spy-given-James-Bond-honour.html.

"Pass from Benedict Arnold for 'John Anderson,' 1780." New York State Archives. Accessed October 11, 2020. http://www.archives.nysed .gov/education/pass-benedict-arnold-john-anderson-1780.

Patterson, Thom. "The Russian Spies Living Next Door." CNN. July 19, 2017. https://www.cnn.com/2017/07/19/us/russian-spies-united -states-declassified/index.html.

Pearlstein, Rick. 2000. "Watergate Scandal." *Encyclopaedia Britannica*. Last modified on June 10, 2020. https://www.britannica.com/event /Watergate-Scandal/Watergate-trial-and-aftermath.

"The People of the CIA...Ames Mole Hunt Team." CIA.gov. Last modified April 30, 2013. https://www.cia.gov/news-information/featured-story -archive/ames-mole-hunt-team.html.

Peterson, Hayley. "Revealed: The Actual Screenplay Drawings behind 'Argo' That Helped American Hostages Escape Iran in 1980." *The Daily Mail*. Last modified February 22, 2013. https://www.dailymail. co.uk/news/article-2282526/Revealed-The-actual-screenplay -drawings-Argo-helped-American-hostages-escape-Iran-1980.html.

Philby, Kim. 1968. *My Silent War: The Autobiography of a Spy*. New York: The Modern Library, 2002.

"Pierre-Augustin Caron de Beaumarchais." Last modified March 15, 2020. https://www.britannica.com/biography/Pierre-Augustin-Caron -de-Beaumarchais.

Pilkington, Ed. "Burglars in 1971 FBI Office Break-In Come Forward after 43 Years." *The Guardian*. January 7, 2014. https://www.theguardian .com/world/2014/jan/07/fbi-office-break-in-1971-come-forward -documents.

"The Playboy Spy Who Inspired James Bond." BBC.com. Video File. March 12, 2020. https://www.bbc.com/reel/video/p086f8jn/the -playboy-serbian-spy-who-inspired-james-bond.

Ponniah, Kevin and Lazara Marinkovic. "The Night the US Bombed a Chinese Embassy." BBC News. May 7, 2019. https://www.bbc.com /news/world-europe-48134881.

Popovici, Alice. "Watergate: Who Did What and Where Are They Now?" History.com. Last modified October 16, 2018. https://www.history .com/news/watergate-where-are-they-now.

"Pots of Fame." *The Economist*. March 31, 2010. https://www.economist .com/books-and-arts/2010/03/31/pots-of-fame.

"Prague Spring." *Encyclopaedia Britannica*. Last modified March 7, 2018. https://www.britannica.com/event/Prague-Spring.

Pressley, Sue Anne. "Group Planned Massacre and Big Robbery, FBI Says." *The Washington Post*. April 25, 1997. https://www.washington post.com/archive/politics/1997/04/25/group-planned-massacre-and -big-robbery-fbi-says/8d864957-b2cf-4c39-be2a-10361b6c31de.

Pruitt, Sarah. "How Codebreakers Helped Secure U.S. Victory in the Battle of Midway." History.com. November 7, 2019. https://www .history.com/news/battle-midway-codebreakers-allies-pacific -theater.

Pruitt, Sarah. "When One of George Washington's Enslaved Workers Escaped to Freedom." History.com. February 18, 2020. https://www .history.com/news/george-washington-and-the-slave-who-got-away.

Ransom, Harry Howe. "Intelligence." *Encyclopaedia Britannica*. Last modified October 16, 2016. https://www.britannica.com/topic /intelligence-international-relations/Russia-and-the-Soviet-Union.

Ray, Michael. "U.S. Secret Service." *Encyclopaedia Britannica*. Last modified February 27, 2020. https://www.britannica.com/topic /US-Secret-Service.

Reagan, Ronald. "President Reagan's 'Evil Empire' Speech to the National Association of Evangelicals." *Making the History of 1989*, item #64. http://chnm.gmu.edu/1989/items/show/64.

Reed, Drew. "Manaus's Opulent Amazon Theatre—a History of Cities in 50 Buildings, Day 15." *The Guardian*. April 14, 2015. https://www .theguardian.com/cities/2015/apr/14/manaus-amazon-theatre-brazil -history-cities-50-buildings.

"Richard I (1157–1199)." BBC.co.uk. Accessed September 24, 2020. http://www.bbc.co.uk/history/historic_figures/richard_i_king.shtml.

Riley, Red. *MI6 Spy Skills for Civilians*. New York: Media Lab Books, 2020.

Rose, Sarah. "The Great British Tea Heist." *Smithsonian Magazine*. March 9, 2010. https://www.smithsonianmag.com/history/the-great -british-tea-heist-9866709.

"Richard I Coeur de Lion ('The Lionheart') (r. 1189–1199)." *The Royal Household*. Accessed October 12, 2020. https://www.royal.uk /richard-i.

Russell, Alec. "CIA Plot Led to Huge Blast in Siberian Gas Pipeline." *The Telegraph*. February 28, 2004. https://www.telegraph.co.uk /news/worldnews/northamerica/usa/1455559/CIA-plot-led-to-huge -blast-in-Siberian-gas-pipeline.html.

Rye, Graham. "Kevin McClory." *The Independent*. December 7, 2006. https://www.independent.co.uk/news/obituaries/kevin-mcclory -427368.html.

"Salisbury Novichok: Second Police Officer Poisoned." BBC News. August 15, 2019. https://www.bbc.com/news/uk-england -wiltshire-49361327.

Savage, Gary. "Favier's Heirs: The French Revolution and the Secret Du Roi." *The Historical Journal* 41, no. 1 (1998): 225–58. www.jstor .org/stable/2640151.

Schöpe, Björn. "Richard the Lionheart Ruins England." *Coins Weekly*. October 14, 2009. https://coinsweekly.com/richard-the-lionheart -ruins-england.

Schumm, Laura. "What Was Operation Paperclip?" History.com. March 4, 2020. https://www.history.com/news/what-was-operation -paperclip.

Seattle Times Staff. "Former Boeing Manager Pleads to Obstruction of Justice in Trade Secrets Case." *The Seattle Times*. December 8, 2006. https://www.seattletimes.com/business/former-boeing -manager-pleads-to-obstruction-in-trade-secrets-case.

Secret Agent. IMDb. Accessed July 5, 2020. https://www.imdb.com
    /title/tt0058846.

Sellers, Robert. "Patrick McGoohan: Actor Who Created and Starred in
    the Cult 1960s Television Series 'The Prisoner.'" *The Independent*.
    February 16, 2009. https://www.independent.co.uk/news/obituaries
    /patrick-mcgoohan-actor-who-created-and-starred-in-the-cult-1960s
    -television-series-the-prisoner-1380371.html.

Siegel, Rachel. "'I Am Ready': Mata Hari Faced a Firing Squad for
    Spying—and Refused a Blindfold." *The Washington Post*. October
    15, 2017. https://www.washingtonpost.com/news/retropolis/
    wp/2017/10/15
    /i-am-ready-mata-hari-faced-a-firing-squad-for-spying-and-refused
    -a-blindfold.

Shakespeare, William. *The Tragedy of Hamlet, Prince of Denmark*.
    Accessed September 24, 2020. http://shakespeare.mit.edu/hamlet
    /full.html.

Shapira, Ian. "'Rick Is a Goddamn Russian Spy': Does the CIA Have a
    New Aldrich Ames on Its Hands?" *The Washington Post*. January
    26, 2018. https://www.washingtonpost.com/news/retropolis/wp
    /2018/01/26/rick-is-a-goddamn-russian-spy-does-the-cia-have-a-new
    -aldrich-ames-on-its-hands.

Shepperson, Mary. "Destruction at the Ancient Site of Mari in Syria."
    The Guardian. April 19, 2018. https://www.theguardian.com
    /science/2018/apr/19/destruction-at-the-ancient-site-of-mari-in-syria.

Smith, David. "Off the Map: The Secret Cities Behind the Atom
    Bomb." *The Guardian*. May 3, 2018. https://www.theguardian.com
    /cities/2018/may/03/off-the-map-the-secret-cities-behind-the-atom
    -bomb-manhattan-project.

Spence, Richard B. *The Real History of Secret Societies—Aleister
    Crowley, Occultism, and Espionage*. TheGreatCourses.com, 2019.
    https://www.thegreatcourses.com/courses/the-real-history-of-secret
    -societies.html.

Swift, John. "Mukden Incident." *Encyclopaedia Britannica*. Last modified September 11, 2019. https://www.britannica.com/event /Mukden-Incident.

Talbert, Richard J. A. "The Role of the Helots in the Class Struggle at Sparta." *Historia: Zeitschrift Für Alte Geschichte* 38, no. 1: 22-40. www.jstor.org/stable/4436088.

"Tea Tuesdays: The Scottish Spy Who Stole China's Tea Empire." NPR.org. March 10, 2015. https://www.npr.org/sections/thesalt/2015 /03/10/392116370/tea-tuesdays-the-scottish-spy-who-stole-chinas -tea-empire.

Tesch, Noah. "Who Were the Assassins?" *Encyclopaedia Britannica*. Accessed June 24, 2020.www.britannica.com/amp/story/who-were -the-assassins.

Thill, Scott. "R.I.P. Patrick McGoohan, *The Prisoner*'s TV Visionary." *Wired*. January 14, 2009. https://www.wired.com/2009/01/rip-patrick -mcg.

Thompson, Jonathan and Nicholas Pyke. "Does the Tomb of St Mark in Venice Really Contain the Bones of Alexander the Great?" *Independent*. June 13, 2004. https://www.independent.co.uk/news /world/europe/does-the-tomb-of-st-mark-in-venice-really-contain -the-bones-of-alexander-the-great-732020.html.

Thucydides. *The History of the Peloponnesian War*. 431 BCE. https://www.gutenberg.org/files/7142/7142-h/7142-h.htm#link2H _4_0015.

"To Catch a Spy: 25th Anniversary of the Aldrich Ames Arrest." CIA.gov. February 19, 2019. https://www.cia.gov/news-information/blog/2019 /to-catch-a-spy-25th-anniversary-of-the-aldrich-ames-arrest.html.

"Trojan War." History.com. Last modified September 11, 2019. https://www.history.com/.amp/topics/ancient-history/trojan-war.

"Twelve Tribes of Israel." *Encyclopaedia Britannica*. Last modified January 31, 2020. https://www.britannica.com/topic/Twelve-Tribes -of-Israel.

Tzu, Sun. *The Art of War*. Translated by Lionel Giles. Accessed September 24, 2020. http://classics.mit.edu/Tzu/artwar.html.

"U-2 Overflights and the Capture of Francis Gary Powers, 1960." US
Department of State Office of the Historian. Accessed July 6, 2020.
https://history.state.gov/milestones/1953-1960/u2-incident.

US Attorney's Office. "Brookline Man Sentenced for Foreign Economic
Espionage." FBI.gov. December 19, 2011. https://archives.fbi.gov
/archives/boston/press-releases/2011/brookline-man-sentenced
-to-for-foreign-economic-espionage.

US Attorney's Office. "Former Boeing Engineer Sentenced to Nearly 16
Years in Prison for Stealing Aerospace Secrets for China." FBI.gov.
February 08, 2010. https://archives.fbi.gov/archives/losangeles
/press-releases/2010/la020810.htm.

US Attorney's Office. "Walter Liew Sentenced to 15 Years in Prison for
Economic Espionage." FBI.gov. July 11, 2014. https://www.fbi.gov
/contact-us/field-offices/sanfrancisco/news/press-releases/walter
-liew-sentenced-to-15-years-in-prison-for-economic-espionage.

Vennard, Martin. "Léon Theremin: The Man and the Music Machine."
BBC News. March 13, 2012. https://www.bbc.com/news/magazine
-17340257.

Virgil. *Aeneid*. Translated by John Dryden. Accessed September 24,
2020. http://classics.mit.edu/Virgil/aeneid.mb.txt.

Weir, Alison. *The Life of Elizabeth I*. New York: Ballantine Books, 1998.

Weiser, Benjamin. "U.S. to Offer Detailed Trail of bin Laden in Bomb
Trial." *New York Times*. January 13, 2001. https://www.nytimes
.com/2001/01/13/nyregion/us-to-offer-detailed-trail-of-bin-laden
-in-bomb-trial.html.

Weiser, Benjamin and Colin Moynihan. "Conduit to Arms Sting, a Star
Witness Apologizes for His Crimes." *New York Times*. May 23, 2012.
https://www.nytimes.com/2012/05/24/nyregion/andrew-smulian
-star-witness-against-viktor-bout-gets-5-years-in-prison.html.

Welsh, Jennifer. "Shark Attack in Egypt? Must Be the Work of Israeli
Agents." *Discover*. December 13, 2010. https://www.discover
magazine.com/planet-earth/shark-attack-in-egypt-must-be-the
-work-of-israeli-agents.

"What We Do." DNI.gov. Accessed June 16 2020. https://www.dni.gov /index.php/what-we-do.

"Year of the Spy (1985)." FBI.gov. Accessed September 24, 2020. https://www.fbi.gov/history/famous-cases/year-of-the-spy-1985.

"The Zimmermann Telegram." Archives.org. Last modified on June 1, 2020. https://www.archives.gov/education/lessons/zimmermann.

Zurawski, Wojciech. "Poles Recall Nazi Seizure of Radio Station, See Parallels with Today." Reuters.com. August 29, 2020. https://www.reuters.com/article/amp/idUSKBN0GT1U820140829.

ACKNOWLEDGMENTS

I'd like to thank Claire Sielaff, Bridget Thoreson, Claire Chun, Renee Rutledge, Mark Rhynsburger, and Rebecca Lown at Ulysses Press for all of their hard work bringing this book to fruition. Also, thanks to everyone else there who labored on it behind the scenes. I couldn't have done this without you. Thanks to the spies and other covert operators, historians, and journalists whose exploits and/or research made this book possible. Also condolences to the families of innocent victims lost due to such activities.

Thanks to my parents, grandparents, teachers, and professors for encouraging me to feed my curiosity about anything and everything.

Thank you, Holly, for putting me through the paces writing technology articles, giving me the chops to write this. Also, thank you for being a friend (cue *Golden Girls* music).

Thanks to my not-quite-twin brother, Daniel, for all the kind words and witty banter that keep me sane.

Thank you, Jeff, for bringing me meals, putting up with me ignoring you for large chunks of time, and being generally awesome.

And thanks to our precious little Molly for barking at me incessantly every time I was on a roll. Okay, maybe that didn't help, but she's cute and gets a pass.

ABOUT THE AUTHOR

Bernadette "Berni" Johnson began her career at age 6, when she crayoned a book about her mom that received a rave review from its lone reader. At 13, she dabbled in computer programming on her Atari 1200, leading to an IT career in adulthood. She holds a BA in English literature and an MA in English with a concentration in humanities computing from the University of Georgia.

Berni combined her tech and wordsmithing skills to write over fifty articles for HowStuffWorks.com. When she's not at the movies, watching TV, or glued to her phone, she studies a variety of topics, reads and writes fiction and nonfiction, and hangs with her partner and their demanding but lovable terrier. You can check out her writing blog at bernijohnson.com.